Praise for *The Transformation Principles*

"*The Transformation Principles* is both timely and essential. In today's world, we are witnessing a paradox—while transformative technologies like AI and GenAI are bringing the world closer, rising geopolitical tensions are causing increasing fragmentation. Navigating this duality requires agility, foresight, and a strong sense of purpose from companies and leaders alike. This book offers a path on how organizations can adapt to uncertainty and complexity without losing sight of the broader goal: inclusive development. It is a must-read for leaders who want to build resilient, future-ready organizations that thrive in a connected yet divided world."
—Natarajan Chandrasekaran, Chairman, Tata Sons

"Hemant Taneja's *The Transformation Principles* is an important read for any leader seeking to create an enduring company. His insights on the importance of being positive, mission-driven, fostering innovation, and embracing a growth mindset are essential for thriving in today's rapidly evolving landscape."
—Adena Friedman, Chair and CEO, Nasdaq

"In a world defined by political, economic, and societal upheaval, leaders are challenged not only to navigate the waves of uncertainty but also to build a lasting legacy. *The Transformation Principles* serves as a guiding light, illuminating the path to innovation that benefits the greater good. In this book, Taneja reveals the secrets to achieving business success while simultaneously creating a positive impact on the world."
—Bill McDermott, Chairman and CEO, ServiceNow

"Principles such as having a soul in business, navigating ambiguity, and embracing radical collaboration are not just strategies for success—they are imperatives for survival in the 21st century. *The Transformation Principles* challenges us to rethink our assumptions, embrace uncertainty, and lead with curiosity and generosity. It is a manifesto for leaders across sectors to build organizations that are not only profitable but also purposeful."

—Bob Sternfels, Global Managing Partner, McKinsey & Company

"Hemant puts words to what the next wave of founders already feel in their gut: building without a soul is a dead end. *The Transformation Principles* is the field manual for building 100-year companies that compound mission, market, and moral purpose. Read it and you'll stop asking 'How do I flip this?' and start asking 'How do I fix the world—and build real lasting abundance for all of us?'"

—Garry Tan, President and CEO, Y Combinator

THE TRANSFORMATION PRINCIPLES

Also by Hemant Taneja and Kevin Maney

Unscaled: How AI and a New Generation of Upstarts Are Creating the Economy of the Future

UnHealthcare: A Manifesto for Health Assurance
(with Stephen Klasko)

Intended Consequences: How to Build Market-Leading Companies with Responsible Innovation

THE TRANSFORMATION PRINCIPLES

How to Create Enduring Change

HEMANT TANEJA

WITH KEVIN MANEY

Matt Holt Books
An Imprint of BenBella Books, Inc.
Dallas, TX

This book is designed to provide accurate and authoritative information about venture capitalism. Neither the author nor the publisher is engaged in rendering legal, accounting, or other professional services by publishing this book. If any such assistance is required, the services of qualified professionals should be sought. The author and publisher will not be responsible for any liability, loss, or risk incurred as a result of the use and application of any information contained in this book.

The Transformation Principles copyright © 2025 by General Catalyst, LLC, and Kevin Maney

All rights reserved. Except in the case of brief quotations embodied in critical articles or reviews, no part of this book may be used or reproduced, stored, transmitted, or used in any manner whatsoever, including for training artificial intelligence (AI) technologies or for automated text and data mining, without prior written permission from the publisher.

Matt Holt is an imprint of BenBella Books, Inc.
8080 N. Central Expressway
Suite 1700
Dallas, TX 75206
benbellabooks.com
Send feedback to feedback@benbellabooks.com

BenBella and *Matt Holt* are federally registered trademarks.

Printed in the United States of America
10 9 8 7 6 5 4 3 2 1

Library of Congress Control Number: 2025022504
ISBN 9781637747353 (hardcover)
ISBN 9781637747360 (electronic)

Editing by Lydia Choi
Copyediting by Scott Calamar
Proofreading by Jenny Bridges and Lisa Story
Text design and composition by Jordan Koluch
Cover design by Natasha Jen, Partner
Cover image © iStock / Ramberg (earth)
Herman Taneja author photo by Jamie Rain/Lunch Break Headshots
Printed by Lakeside Book Company

Special discounts for bulk sales are available.
Please contact bulkorders@benbellabooks.com.

*To my partner and mentor, Ken Chenault,
for guiding me in my quest to redefine capitalism
as a driver of inclusive and sustainable society.*

—*Hemant*

Contents

Foreword   xi

INTRODUCTION	The Case for the Transformation Principles	1
CHAPTER ONE	The Business Must Have a Soul	29
CHAPTER TWO	Navigating Ambiguity Is More Valuable Than Predicting the Future	47
CHAPTER THREE	Creating the Future Beats Improving the Past	65
CHAPTER FOUR	Those Who Play Their Own Game Win	81
CHAPTER FIVE	Serendipity Must Become Intentional	97
CHAPTER SIX	For Great Change, Radical Collaboration Beats Disruption	115
CHAPTER SEVEN	Context Constantly Changes, but Human Nature Stays the Same	135
CHAPTER EIGHT	The Choice Between Positive Impact and Returns Is False	159
CHAPTER NINE	The Best Results Come from Leading with Curiosity and Generosity	175
EPILOGUE	How the Transformation Principles Apply to AI	191

Acknowledgments   211

Notes   213

Foreword

By now it is clear that the economic system that reigned supreme for the past three decades is under strain. Liberalization, openness, and speed all had great advantages. But a series of global shocks—chief among them the 2008 financial crisis, COVID-19, and rising geopolitical tensions—has laid bare the vulnerabilities of a system based around interconnection. A new brand of populist politics has proliferated across the globe, with a deep skepticism of the neoliberal economics that dominated the world since the late twentieth century. Where once a consensus stood around free markets and free trade, a new consensus is forming around national resilience and protectionism to varying degrees. Whether this is the ideal economic system is in some ways irrelevant. Political and social pressures are converging around new sets of ideas. While the exact shape of this new consensus is still being determined, it is clearly a departure from the old one.

It is precisely with this understanding of our current moment that Hemant Taneja makes his important intervention with *The*

Foreword

Transformation Principles. The task at hand is daunting: If the current economic system is approaching an impasse, what should replace it? And if capitalism is to survive through the rest of this century and beyond, how should it evolve?

Taneja begins by taking a step back to understand the complexity of our current order. What the world experienced under this economic system has been nothing short of extraordinary. After the collapse of the Soviet Union, American policy preferences were adopted around the world, and governments made major macroeconomic and political reforms along the lines of what came to be known as the "Washington Consensus." As Margaret Thatcher famously quipped about her neoliberal reforms, there was simply "no alternative." Policies were designed to unleash market forces—including deregulation, financial privatization, and low trade barriers across nations. This helped fuel the world's first truly open economic system, enabling globalization to soar to new heights with the free flow of goods, services, and people across borders.

The world of technology flourished in this era, too, powered by global connectivity, open technology platforms, and minimal regulation. In 1989, as the world fixated on turmoil in the Soviet Union, an equally transformative shift was taking place on the other side of Europe, in Geneva: The CERN lab had developed the foundations of the modern internet. This inaugurated the era of information technology and created an entire new digital economy, one based on bits and bytes instead of atoms. Ideas spread more quickly around the world, and the global economy became even more interconnected, facilitating the rise of global value chains. Companies spread production processes across multiple countries and leveraged new technologies globally. Innovative

Foreword

startups came onto the scene, disrupting the global market with low barriers to entry.

All of this created a world that was overall more unified, more productive, and more prosperous, raising standards of living for all. Since 1990, over one billion people have been lifted out of poverty, with the share of the global population living below $2.15 per day—today's international poverty line—falling from 38% in 1990 to 9% in 2022. Global inflation-adjusted GDP per capita has more than doubled over that same period, jumping from $8,211 in 1990 to $16,677 in 2022. In many developing countries, economic growth rates have even outpaced those seen in advanced economies during their industrial revolutions. Global life expectancy increased 15 years over the past half century, and literacy rates soared more than 20%. Thanks to expanded access to education, almost 90% of the world can now read and write. Advances in medicine, sanitation, and nutrition have led to better health outcomes globally, and many diseases that were once common causes of death have now been eradicated.

Yet for all of the wealth and progress the open international system generated, these benefits have not always been felt equally. Certain sectors, such as manufacturing in heartland America, have been hollowed out from automation and offshoring. Real wages for low- and middle-income workers have stagnated in many developed countries, contributing to rising income inequality. Most fundamentally, communities have experienced rapid disruptions as local stores and associations have been replaced by online ones, leaving individuals feeling unmoored and left behind. The period of breakneck capitalism, globalization, and the information revolution have served the world well. But they have also demonstrated the need for economic shock absorbers

Foreword

to balance the volatility of market forces and anchor individuals. Moving forward, a new approach is required—one that promotes economic resilience, not solely pure growth.

Taneja grasps the significance of this inflection point and lays a path forward. He explains how, for much of the twentieth century, the prevailing model of capitalism focused predominantly on short-term profits. While the relentless pursuit of profit indeed lifted billions out of poverty and extended lifespans significantly, it also exacerbated social, political, and environmental divides. According to Taneja, the era of profit-only capitalism has run its course and is not equipped to tackle the longer horizons of today's problems, from health inequities to climate change. Instead, he proposes that a new paradigm, one he terms inclusive capitalism, should take its place. Inclusive capitalism differs from profit-only capitalism in that it recognizes the fundamental link between business and society. It promotes financial success and societal well-being at the same time.

At the heart of this book are the nine transformation principles that Taneja has developed and implemented over his many years leading the global venture capital company General Catalyst. They are intuitive yet illuminating insights, ranging from technical investment strategies to philosophical accounts of human nature. Overall, these principles are meant to serve as a road map for creating a new kind of company. They challenge the traditional venture capital mindset that prioritizes quick exits over sustainable growth, and which contrives a false dichotomy between financial and social benefits. Companies can, and should, aim for both.

Taneja instructs leaders in the venture capital industry to fund and scale the "businesses of tomorrow" by cultivating and

Foreword

adhering to a core set of principles. We learn through his personal accounts of companies like Merck and Airbnb that guiding principles are not antithetical to financial success but often the very foundation of it. This will only become truer for companies that aim to leverage technologies like AI, blockchain, and synthetic biology. These emerging technologies have the potential to massively improve lives around the world; but without a principled approach, they can also exacerbate existing divides or create new ones. Similarly, these technologies can be immensely valuable once they are widely adopted and transform entire industries; but this will only occur if they are first aligned with societal values. Taneja's ideas could lead businesses to adopt a new and different mindset, and if that happens, they might stave off pressures to add new regulations to the roster, which always come with the danger of inefficiency, corruption, and market distortion.

With each of his transformation principles, Taneja is keenly aware that what made businesses successful in the previous era will no longer suffice. As a new economic consensus emerges, companies will need to reorient themselves accordingly. Governments are now taking a more prominent role in the private sector, making it such that businesses can no longer operate in complete isolation and expect to radically disrupt things. They will need to work in tandem with state institutions and civil society and innovate responsibly. Put simply, if companies want to achieve lasting success in this new era, they will need to focus on building for the long term and move beyond the old Silicon Valley mantra of "move fast and break things."

The book's real lasting power comes from the fact that its lessons can be applied far beyond the business realm. We are not only living through major economic shifts but also profound

Foreword

psychological ones. Around the world, there seems to be a crisis in meaning, with people desperately searching for a cause to fill the void that religion once did. In *The Transformation Principles*, we are reminded that this purpose can in fact be self-created. For Taneja, it is about building a world where business and societal interests align, where innovation serves the greater good, and where companies can achieve lasting success by doing what is right.

—Fareed Zakaria, New York, 2024

INTRODUCTION

THE CASE FOR THE TRANSFORMATION PRINCIPLES

Capitalism has long been a system focused solely on generating profits, usually in the short term. That focus did a lot of good in the twentieth century. Businesses built global consumer economies and lifted billions of people out of poverty and into the middle class. Improved standards of living have added decades to lifespans since 1900.

But in the twenty-first century, the supremacy of short-term profits coupled with an extraordinary explosion of powerful technologies are creating ever-growing divides. Wealth has accrued to the top 1% while leaving behind large swaths of people everywhere in the world. That's led to social and political divides that are polarizing societies. Advances in medicine and genomics tend to benefit the rich, opening a health divide.[1] Climate change is accelerating and is creating climate divides as many regions see water shortages, severe weather, and challenged agriculture.

That's not an indictment of capitalism. It's an indictment of *profit-only capitalism*, which has run its course and will now do more damage than good. If we're going to harness the powerful technologies we're now developing—especially artificial intelligence—to broadly improve our lives and give us stable, thriving societies for the long term, we need a new brand of capitalism: *inclusive capitalism*.

Inclusive capitalism focuses on returns plus impact. It understands that every company and product are part of a societal system and must contribute to the vitality of that system. It is still capitalism. I believe capitalism is the best way to bring innovation and progress to the world, and responsible innovation is the best way for us to fix the problems and divides we now live with. Yet while profit-only capitalism was a force for positive progress in the last century, inclusive capitalism must be the force for positive progress in this one. And, as I'll show, inclusive capitalism is now the best way to generate exceptional, enduring returns.

Some might think that inclusive capitalism is some radical new idea, but it is not. The concept in various forms has been with us for most of civilization. In his 2024 book *The Greatest of All Plagues*, political science professor David Lay Williams makes the case that Plato, Jesus, Thomas Hobbes, Jean-Jacques Rousseau, Adam Smith, and John Stuart Mill all saw great economic divides as a massive threat to societies (i.e., "the greatest plague"). The remedy for dangerous divides, Williams concludes, has always been a system that lets everyone more broadly benefit from economic, technological, and political successes.[2]

Today, inclusive capitalism requires a new mindset for company building, investment, and wealth creation. This is particularly needed in my industry of venture capital (VC) and across the startup ecosystem. We're the ones funding, starting, and scaling the companies of the future, so we need to operate by a new set of principles—*transformation principles*.

Developing, practicing, and evangelizing such principles is

The Case for the Transformation Principles

now my raison d'être. In this book, I detail nine principles that have profoundly influenced my company, General Catalyst. We are developing a new category of venture capital. It is a platform that allows us to activate the best founders to build category-defining companies as early as possible (this is our core, early-stage VC), activate ecosystems of innovation, partner with industry (like our health assurance partnerships), and drive sustainable and inclusive transformations of major industries. We intend to build on a movement that takes investing and company building from "financial *or* societal benefit" to "financial *and* societal benefit"—from "exit" as the only endgame to "endure" as a preferred endgame. We believe that great returns and enduring positive impact go together and feed each other. Living and working with these transformation principles isn't just a strategy that's good for society—it's the best strategy for building a good business.

This flips the script on the way business has often operated. Too many business leaders—now and in the past—have assumed that they can reap the profits of disruption and then repent through philanthropy. All too often, corporate leaders have used the language of philanthropy, corporate social responsibility (CSR), and environmental, social, and governance (ESG) to mitigate or obfuscate harm otherwise caused by a company's practices. We need to break this mindset and make sure companies build for impact plus returns from the start.

In the coming decade or two, companies that operate for impact plus returns will financially perform far better than companies that remain stuck in the traditional profit-only capitalism model. Companies and investors that dismiss inclusive capitalism will find themselves on the wrong side of history.

Here are the nine transformation principles for investing,

The Transformation Principles

innovating, and company building. In the coming chapters, I'll dive deeply into each.

1. The business must have a soul.
2. Navigating ambiguity is more valuable than predicting the future.
3. Creating the future beats improving the past.
4. Those who play their own game win.
5. Serendipity must become intentional.
6. For great change, radical collaboration beats disruption.
7. Context constantly changes, but human nature stays the same.
8. The choice between positive impact and returns is false.
9. The best results come from leading with curiosity and generosity.

I also believe these principles can guide anyone who wants to transform anything, whether it's a nation, an industry, a company, a family, or themselves. As you'll see, I don't just conduct business guided by these principles—I live them, and I first learned them through life and spiritual lessons.

The times we live in are the reason we need such principles. We're at a moment when powerful technologies and historic geopolitical shifts are remaking whole industries and the world economy. Navigate this period wisely, and we'll have a chance to make the world a far better place. Do this in an unprincipled way, and we can make things much worse.

The Case for the Transformation Principles

Tomorrow's most important technology companies will impact billions of lives and livelihoods in ever more profound ways as we seek to become a true digital society and reorganize all aspects of life and business online. We are in the middle of a 30-year technology cycle that started around 2007 with the introduction of the iPhone and the explosion of cloud computing. Now the transformational technologies we're developing, most significantly artificial intelligence (AI), are improving at such a furious pace that society seems to have little time to respond to its consequences. Alongside AI, the technologies of robotics, blockchain, genomics, virtual reality, and 3D printing are all racing into our lives.

General Catalyst has been investing in AI-driven companies for years—Livongo for diabetes, Grammarly for language, and Applied Intuition for automobiles. (More on all of those later.) Now we're taking this new powerful AI and applying it to transform industries. AI (with the addition of some of the other foundational technologies) can give us the means to reinvent healthcare into health assurance, giving everyone personalized ways to stay healthy, manage chronic conditions, and get treated at home so they can stay out of hospitals. AI will be used to reinvent transportation, giving us highly safe driverless electric vehicles that replace gas-powered cars and trucks, with big climate and safety benefits. (The end of drunk driving!) AI will have similar profound effects on every industry and every kind of work, at its best freeing humans from the mundane so we can focus on the creative and sublime. If implemented using sound principles, these technologies can drive incredible positive change that brings everyone along in an inclusive and equitable way.

And that's critically important. The last time we went through

The Transformation Principles

such a transformational tech cycle was from around 1890 to 1920, when electricity, the telephone, automobiles, and airplanes burst onto the scene. Life in 1890 was completely changed by 1920. Similarly, life before 2007 will seem almost unrecognizable by 2037. And so much change drives fear, as people wonder how new technology will impact them and whether it will make them irrelevant. While automation in the past has often replaced the work of human hands, this new wave threatens the work of human minds. Lawyers, accountants, writers, software coders, and those in many other professions have to wonder about their futures. If we generate too much uncertainty too quickly—if it is perceived that we are letting AI and its parallel technologies destroy without rebuilding—we will wind up with a society in turmoil.

As of this writing, the tech industry and governments all over the world are debating how or whether to manage the development of AI. One camp is taking the "let 'er rip" approach, advocating for letting the technology move fast and break things. But AI is so powerful, it threatens to break too many things too fast, which will invite heavy regulation and whip up societal backlash. In the long run, developing AI in an unguided, unprincipled way will slow it down, not speed it up. The transformation principles in this book guide us to a different approach. By working with leaders in government and industry to make sure AI has a positive impact, we have a better chance of building successful, enduring AI-driven companies. AI that benefits us all will develop faster if we take on a shared responsibility to develop it for impact plus returns.

If you doubt that's true, look at what happened when the world applied the "let 'er rip" approach to cryptocurrencies. In the 2010s, crypto seemed to have enormous promise. Many thought

The Case for the Transformation Principles

it could be used to create a more resilient, inclusive form of banking, or a global currency immune to transfer fees or the whims of central banks. Now such dreams are stalled. Volatile cryptocurrencies have too often crashed and gutted the finances of millions of people. Bitcoin farms are sucking up more electricity than some cities and adding to global warming. The founder of crypto company FTX, Sam Bankman-Fried, wound up convicted of seven counts of defrauding his customers and was sentenced to 25 years in prison, while FTX has gone bankrupt. If AI is similarly unmoored, it risks getting similarly reined in by regulators, the courts, and the public, which would be a loss. Blockchain is an important technology, and a more responsible approach would have accelerated its progress and the building of beneficial crypto-based companies.

We can't afford to repeat the mistakes of recent decades. While our industry ushered in one of the greatest periods of innovation and investment in human history, its legacy is that we lack inclusive prosperity while we have eroded respectful society and threatened our planet. Founders and venture capitalists have too often abdicated responsibility for the impact of the companies our investments helped create. Since the boom years of venture capital starting in the 1990s, we've tended to think our only job is to spawn companies, disrupt markets, deliver strong returns for our limited partners (aka investors), and pile up personal wealth for ourselves. We've assumed society would figure out the rest. But it hasn't, and that's a danger. As history shows, enormous divides lead to unrest and cracks in society's foundation. The worse that gets, the worse the environment becomes for business of any kind.

At the same time, we're seeing the confluence of three innovation megatrends that are building on each other and reshaping

The Transformation Principles

society, adding to the urgency to embrace inclusive capitalism and enduring positive change.

The first is the ongoing digital transformation I described: the 30-year cycle of innovation that is reorganizing all of society online.

That, in turn, is leading to the second megatrend: workforce transformation with AI. Every CEO in every boardroom in every industry is discussing what to do with AI. It will have a profound effect on the livelihoods of billions of workers. What's at stake is the very nature of work and of human purpose.

It's not just companies that will have to manage massive workforce transformation—this will affect whole nations and realign economic relationships. Look, for instance, at customer service contact centers. Over the past 30 years, US companies have sent hundreds of thousands of contact center jobs abroad, relying on less-expensive employees in places like India, the Philippines, and Jamaica. AI systems are already becoming good enough to interact with customers by voice in a way that seems nearly human—and sometimes better, because AI can learn every response to every common question. It never forgets and never has to click around on a keyboard to find an answer. A major contact center might have 100,000 employees. AI could make most of those jobs unnecessary, retaining a relatively small base of experts to handle problems AI can't. I call this "AI onshoring"—bringing the contact center back to the home country with software. The leaders of nations that will lose these jobs will need a strategy to manage this shift or risk great societal disruption. The flip side is that AI also brings the promise of, for instance, upskilling millions of people with inexpensive, high-quality AI tutors, giving them a chance to get better-paying, more rewarding jobs. How this all

The Case for the Transformation Principles

plays out and how well or poorly the transition is managed will have weighty consequences around the world.

Finally, there's the third megatrend: We're seeing a geopolitical transformation of critical industries. Countries are rethinking their most essential industries and services and investing for greater resilience in key sectors such as defense, intelligence, infrastructure, supply chain, and energy.

Look at it this way—if you are the leader of a country today, you have to be thinking: *Do we really want to rely on the United States for the vaccine for the next pandemic? Or are we going to build our own capability?* Similar dynamics are driving a global rethink about energy independence, defense, all the critical industries. We also see a re-globalization of manufacturing. In recent decades, businesses everywhere moved manufacturing to China and other places where there is labor arbitrage, taking advantage of cost efficiencies. Now companies are moving to disengage from suppliers in some of those countries and re-engage with a friendlier ecosystem. The United States, Europe, and India are coalescing into one ecosystem while another is forming around China plus its affiliates. So, how do companies create new, resilient supply chains without interrupting their operations?

These will be some of the biggest innovations our industry can work on, and they require a mindset of collaboration between the tech ecosystem, incumbents, and policymakers, as well as a better understanding of how things will play out over longer time horizons.[3]

If the innovation ecosystem is going to play a responsible role in these megatrends, we need a new playbook for how we operate.

The Transformation Principles

Adhering to transformation principles doesn't mean the old and tested tools of business are invalid. Over the past 50 years, when investors and founders have built companies, they've typically looked at businesses through financial, strategic, and operational lenses. All are still essential. But we must add a societal impact lens, asking: Is this company poised to make an important, enduring impact and, therefore, generate compounding returns over the long haul?

By the way, today's most talented people want to work for returns-plus-impact companies. That trend will further compound the competitive advantage of such companies and improve their chances of enduring and generating outsize returns. Fake impact won't cut it—talented people see through it. They will increasingly look for companies that bake real impact into their business models. Consumers, too, want to buy from impact companies. In B2B settings, businesses also want to work with impact companies.

Operating by a set of deeply held principles is not a new, radical, or anti-capitalist idea. Some of the greats in business have leaned on a set of principles and flourished because of it.

In 1963, IBM CEO Thomas Watson Jr. published an influential book titled *A Business and Its Beliefs*. The company at the time was 50 years old and a year away from introducing the System/360 computer, which would set in motion the greatest run of growth, at the time, in US corporate history. In three sentences in his book, Watson laid out the case for operating by principles—or, to use his term, beliefs:

> I firmly believe that any organization, in order to survive and achieve success, must have a sound set of beliefs on which it premises all its policies and actions. Next, I believe that the

The Case for the Transformation Principles

most important single factor in corporate success is faithful adherence to those beliefs. And finally, I believe that if an organization is to meet the challenges of a changing world, it must be prepared to change everything about itself except those beliefs.[4]

IBM faltered in the 1990s and lost its position as a tech industry superstar, and many have argued that this was because the company drifted away from its beliefs.

In a more personal way, I've been exposed to the power of the principles that have long guided the pharmaceutical giant Merck. Ken Frazier joined General Catalyst as chairman of Health Assurance Initiatives after he retired as CEO of Merck. For more than 130 years, Merck has made decisions about its business based on its revered *ethos*—another term for a set of principles.

As Ken has told me, the Merck ethos starts with a commitment to science excellence. While many big pharma companies have essentially become marketers of drugs that are licensed from smaller research-focused drug developers, Merck has maintained a $12 billion to $14 billion (and sometimes more) research and development budget and strives to have the best pharma lab in the world. Equally important is the company's principle of "patients first."

George W. Merck, president of the company from 1925 to 1950, was famously quoted in the August 18, 1952, issue of *Time* magazine saying, "Medicine is for the people, not for the profits." Merck believes in doing what's right for the patients who use its drugs, even if it causes short-term financial pain for the company. In the early 2000s, that led to Merck pulling the best-selling drug Vioxx from the market when a long-term study the

The Transformation Principles

company conducted showed Vioxx can increase the risk of heart problems. The decision cost Merck billions in revenue and lawsuit settlements. But as Ken says, it was the right thing to do for Merck's long-term success. The ethos also embeds in Merck the idea that the company exists for societal good—a principle that guided its decision to give away its river blindness drug to help populations that could never have afforded to pay for it. How has all this played out for the company and its shareholders? Merck's stock in February 1983 was worth about two dollars. In April 2024, it passed $127—with a valuation of $324 billion.

Of course, history is full of many unprincipled companies that generated great returns over long periods of time. These include oil companies, tobacco companies, soft drink companies, and, yes, some modern tech companies. But times have changed. Consumer and investor attitudes have changed. Companies that do harm to the planet, society, or individuals will have a harder time generating good returns. They'll bleed talent. They'll find themselves hauled in front of courts and Congress. (Companies that operate seemingly devoid of principles can spectacularly crash and burn. Think Enron, WorldCom, or AIG.)

Why is a set of principles so effective for a business? When they permeate throughout a company, from its leaders to its foot soldiers, they become a kind of invisible hand guiding every decision. Not unlike the beliefs and moral codes of a religion, sound principles embed a filter that guides behavior. Technology will always rapidly change. The world we operate in will change. As IBM's Tom Watson Jr. would put it, the way to navigate all of that change is to stay true to your principles and be willing to let go of everything else.

The Case for the Transformation Principles

Importantly, a set of principles also sets a person or organization free to approach decisions with a *beginner's mind*.

A lot of people seek to become experts in something, and society needs them. These are the people who spend their lives deeply understanding and working on, for instance, quantum physics, or skyscraper engineering, or heart surgery.

But there can be a downside to expertise. It can become a lens that is something like a telescope: powerful but narrow. Your beliefs are shaped by what you know, and so maybe you "know" that something can't be done, so you don't try to do it—or "know" that there is an established best way to do things and so don't challenge it.

While we need experts, we also need others who don't have the bias of an expert—who look at something with a beginner's mind and think, *Well, maybe that impossible thing can be done, or maybe there is a better way to do things.* It's an anti-pattern way of looking at the world. In the VC industry, we discuss pattern recognition a lot, but in reality, it's the outliers that drive the greatest returns. Exponential success isn't conventional—instead, it arises out of a product or business that seems, at first, weird and mind-bending. A beginner's mind doesn't pollute a weird or mind-bending idea with thoughts of the conventional. A beginner's mind forces humility: You don't know what's possible, so why not explore and find out?

The big breakthroughs—the companies that show us a new way to live or work—typically come from people who have a beginner's mind. There's a reason Airbnb was not started by a hotel

The Transformation Principles

veteran, why Uber wasn't started by a taxi company, and why Warby Parker wasn't started by a major eyeglass maker.

Principles are like scaffolding for a beginner's mind. They are based on the physics of enduring businesses. In practice, principles become rules for seeing every opportunity in a fresh way. For investors, instead of starting with questions about financials and total addressable market, a beginner's mind wants to start with a narrative, asking: *Why did you start this company?* It wants to know what future this founder sees that the rest of us don't. It wants to know if the leadership team can learn and adapt, because if they are trying something that hasn't been done, they will run into dead ends, zigzags, and discoveries they never expected.

At General Catalyst, we've been remaking ourselves into an institution that is guided by our transformation principles. We believe that tomorrow's most financially successful, compounding businesses will be those that operate in the best interests of society. The best-performing investment organization is defined by having the best-performing investments, and those are the ones that compound for a long time—and businesses only get to compound for a long time if they operate in the interest of society.

My journey to discover and define nine transformation principles started with a mindset of spirituality, and that led to our work to transform our company, venture capital, and healthcare.

I can trace my spiritual mindset back to my childhood in India, attending a tiny tin-roofed school in Delhi where we learned Hinduism and read Vedic philosophy alongside studies in math, science, and history. In other words, at my school spirituality was

The Case for the Transformation Principles

not separate from "real-world" subjects; it was a lens—a filter—through which to understand those subjects in relation to societal well-being and a sense of self-mastery. The goal was always to use one's powers to do good in the world.

Even if you weren't brought up in the Hindu religion, you probably know that Hindus believe in the eternal nature of the soul—in other words, reincarnation. One's life on Earth is but a chapter in a soul's journey; your soul has had a long path before you were born into this body, and you will have a long path after this body is gone. So Hinduism encourages thought processes in the context of the long term—doing things in this life in the context of many lives. Each lifetime is but a chapter in the enduring journey of your soul. There is no fear of loss because you are just moving to new reincarnations. I have failed so many times in my three professional decades, but Hindu beliefs have allowed me to be calm and absorb the highs and lows. I try to instill that kind of sensibility in founders I work with to help them face so much uncertainty and risk.

Enduring businesses have a soul with multiple lives through generations of leaders. Look at American Express, for instance. By having a soul guided by core values, it could morph with the times, starting as a freight forwarding company in 1850 (hence the company name), leveraging that into traveler's checks to help its customers keep their money safe while in foreign countries, and then moving on to the travel business, credit cards, and financial services. A company's long-term success depends more on its core beliefs than on the products it sells at any given moment.

Spirituality—aided, as I've found, by meditation—is integral to understanding the larger global system that we're all building and are responsible for. It encourages thinking intentionally and being mindful of consequences. It helps manage the tension between immediate demands and the future good. It provides fuel for endurance. People who work and think this way are the ones who, more often than not, build great, lasting companies.

Stephen Covey famously described one of his seven habits of highly effective people as: "Begin with the end in mind." I believe that spiritual leaders understand that there is no end. Better to begin as if there is no end. To paraphrase the Bhagavad Gita: *Focus on the journey, not the fruits of your labor.*

To be such an enduring leader, you need to understand yourself, understand your place in the universe, develop and apply skills that allow you to make a difference, and harmonize your work with the interests of society and the universe. For me, getting to that point has taken a lifetime of probing, failing, discovering, and learning.

When I was in ninth grade in India, my father got a job in the United States, and a year later my family moved to Brookline, Massachusetts. The day we got there, my father was laid off, leaving us in financial difficulty. We lived in a basement apartment, and I slept next to the boiler. To help the family, I worked 20 to 30 hours a week at a CVS while going to high school. And I was a happy kid. The school was a wonder to me. In India, students have no choice of courses. In the United States, I was allowed to follow my curiosity and learn what I wanted to learn. I sped through schoolwork, studying in between CVS shifts. I went from a kid in India studying, taking naps, and playing cricket to a kid with

The Case for the Transformation Principles

a jammed schedule of school, work, and assimilating into a new culture in America.

After high school, I got accepted into the Massachusetts Institute of Technology (MIT). Freshman year, I got a D on my first exam in organic chemistry. Quite a wake-up call. There were many students at MIT who were smarter than me and were doing everything they could to get straight As. Soon, I started seeing that as odd. Most of us had come to MIT to have outlier success, but so many students got caught in the conventional pattern of driving toward a degree and getting straight As. I decided then to be *different* from them. I followed my curiosity and took every course that looked interesting to me instead of managing my academic credentials. I became like a greedy algorithm, programmed to always do the most interesting thing I could be doing at any given time. This led to an interesting situation: I got close to getting degrees in a whole lot of majors but not enough to graduate with a single degree. I decided to suffer during my last couple of years and complete as many degrees as I could—and ended up with five different ones. I find it embarrassing that people talk about my five degrees from MIT . . . but it's also interesting that nobody cares what grades I got. All in all, playing my own game has paid off and led me to this principle: *Those who play their own game win.*

Early in my career, a classmate, Ken Zolot, and I created a class in MIT's engineering school called Founder's Journey. The technologists at MIT at the time were not being taught how to be entrepreneurs—how to connect tech disciplines to business disciplines. I believed more people should be exposed to the opportunity to start companies. That course was taken by the eventual

The Transformation Principles

founders of Stripe, Segment, and other successful startups. I met the Stripe and Segment founders while teaching the course and decided to fund their startups. The course is still being taught today.

In 1999, I started my first company, Isovia, with a group of MIT friends. As is often said, there's a lot to be learned from failure, and as a first-time entrepreneur, I failed. We started the company for the wrong reasons. It was the height of the dot-com bubble of the late 1990s. We were watching a lot of successful companies get created and wanted to do the same. We had no emotional connection to the product we were building—we started a company for the sake of having a startup. That was our first mistake. Our company didn't have a soul.

Second mistake with Isovia: It was during the prehistoric era of smartphones, and we developed software to make it easy to build applications for those smartphones. But we were trying to replicate, on phones, applications that were already on the web. We never thought to reimagine apps that would take advantage of the phone and mobility. Our business didn't work because we were replicating the past instead of imagining a new future. Isovia's failure led me to understand another principle: *Creating the future beats improving the past.* The future would eventually arrive in 2007 in the form of Apple's iPhone, but by the time it came out, my company had long disappeared into an acquisition.

After we sold that company, I got invited to be an entrepreneur in residence at General Catalyst, which was then just a year old and based in Boston, founded by Joel Cutler and David Fialkow. It wasn't long before they invited me to join GC full-time as an investor, and I felt honored that they let me invest in their companies. The first investment I made was in a company called

The Case for the Transformation Principles

Site Advisor, founded by my friend Chris Dixon, now a VC at Andreessen Horowitz.

The idea was to create "safe search." It was difficult in the internet's early years to know if you were going to land on a credible website or on a site that was going to riddle your computer with pop-up ads or spyware. People will do bad things anywhere they can. In real life, if you were to walk into a bad neighborhood, you'd quickly understand you might not be safe. But there were no such clues on the internet. Site Advisor would let you know if a site was safe before you clicked. Through this work, I came to understand the principle: *Context constantly changes, but human nature stays the same.* This principle about human nature is at the heart of one of my previous books, *Intended Consequences: How to Build Market-Leading Companies with Responsible Innovation,* and my establishment of Responsible Innovation Labs. In order for companies to endure and make a positive impact, they must be mindful of human nature—the good and the bad—and avoid harmful unintended consequences.

I spent my first years at General Catalyst learning to spot trends and invest in companies, and then I'd hope that I had picked the right ones. It's how most VCs operate today. But I found investing this way unrewarding and unsustainable. Latching on to trends made me a follower. I was trying to invest in what others were investing in. That wasn't playing my own game, or creating a future, or backing someone whose soul was devoted to a mission. I wasn't working with a beginner's mind, taking on things others thought couldn't be done.

So I started to apply my emerging transformation principles. I began investing in energy technology to try to have an effect on climate change, at a time when climate tech was barely a thing.

The Transformation Principles

But sectors like energy (or healthcare or finance) are enormous and complex, and they are careful about change. Energy executives don't want new technology bringing down the electric grid. So my investments had disappointing impacts, but the disappointments taught me another of the principles in this book: *For great change, radical collaboration beats disruption.* The way to change a massive, complex industry is not to "disrupt" the old way. Better to work with the incumbent companies and policymakers as a partner, helping them create change throughout the ecosystem.

By 2011, I'd moved into a leadership position at General Catalyst. We realized that to be a significant player in tech, we had to be in Silicon Valley. So I moved my family there, including my parents, and General Catalyst opened an office in Palo Alto. By then I had learned to invest based on some of the principles in this book, evaluating opportunities with a beginner's mind. That proved key when making an investment in Stripe, which would have an enormous impact on General Catalyst and my career.

Many other investors who knew a lot about online payments passed on Stripe, wondering why the world needed another company in what seemed like a commoditized space. But by looking with a beginner's mind, I wasn't swayed by conventional wisdom, and so it struck me when Stripe's founders, Patrick and John Collison, said they wanted to develop a platform that would be the foundation for e-commerce companies built by entrepreneurs not even born yet. As of this writing, Stripe is one of the most valuable tech companies started in the past 15 years. General Catalyst has participated in almost every fundraising round of Stripe's existence, and in aggregate Stripe is the biggest investment in the history of our company.

In 2014, I traveled back to Boston to meet with Joel and

The Case for the Transformation Principles

David. I'd gained confidence as an investor, and my experiences in the Bay Area had convinced me that venture capital and the way innovation would get built was changing. I saw an opportunity for General Catalyst to change with it and build something more impactful. GC had started out as entrepreneurs helping entrepreneurs. I felt we needed to grow into a more intentional, well-run business, with a structure and plan for the future. But it was their firm, so I asked them if they'd let me drive that shift for GC. The alternative would be that I'd transition out of GC and go out on my own. To my positive surprise, they didn't even blink. They told me to go for it.

So we all thought about the culture we should create to build an enduring entity. And we took inspiration from well-run companies we admired, like Stripe and others in our portfolio. And we needed a more ambitious goal than just investing in companies. We came to believe our goal would be to transform whole industries.

Around the same time, everything I experienced at General Catalyst seemed to be confirming that venture capital—and capitalism itself—had to go through a shift from focusing on maximizing short-term returns to maximizing enduring positive change. It became obvious that important technologies like AI and blockchain were going to be used to reinvent every industry. I wrote the book *Unscaled* to describe how new inventions were going to dismantle the scaled-up industries of the twentieth century and create a new unscaled economy in the twenty-first.

I also understood that I had a lot of lucky breaks that took me from a tiny school in India to the contributions I'm able to make today. How many others don't get those breaks—and so don't have the wherewithal to build a company or create a breakthrough?

The Transformation Principles

That kind of thinking led to my belief in inclusive capitalism. If vastly more people have access to a good education, stable living conditions, decent healthcare, and loans or funding, we will get many more companies that create value and jobs and improve our lives. This idea is supported by Vedic philosophy, which focuses on inputs rather than outputs. If society delivers on the inputs (better opportunity for more people), we will get positive outputs (more great, enduring companies that benefit society).

Because of all the tech and societal trends described in this introduction, this is the time to invest in tech companies that deliver powerful, positive change over the long term. Our company is convinced that the best path to great returns and profound outcomes will come from making our investment decisions through the filter of our transformation principles.

My company and I have been on a journey to codify and operate by these transformation principles. My personal success is the result of implicitly or explicitly following these principles, and my deep conviction is that we are on a path to building a category-defining investment company that alters the nature of capitalism. When I look at our biggest drivers of returns—by companies such as Stripe, Livongo, and Samsara—their leaders deeply care about and follow the transformation principles. And following them has served General Catalyst well: Over the past 20 years, the company's assets under management (AUM) have grown from $257 million to $33.2 billion as of late 2024. We started as a regional Boston VC and now operate nine offices globally, including in Silicon Valley, New York, London, Berlin, and Mumbai.

The Case for the Transformation Principles

We're deep into the process of building a company that marries an engine of innovation (operating on a venture capital time frame) to an engine of transformation (operating on indefinite time frames). The concept is to take the risks of investing in startups, but instead of looking to get our money out by exiting those that succeed, we will invest in making sure those companies endure and have a meaningful and responsible impact. We can then reinvest those enduring returns into more innovation, creating a flywheel effect of constantly turning the serendipity of innovation into the intentionality of endurance.

We're transforming ourselves into a new category of business, following our own principles of playing our own game, creating a new future, and focusing on returns plus impact. By the time you read this, we will barely be recognizable as a venture capital entity. We'll be a global investment and transformation company that invests in emerging innovations, starts our own businesses, builds companies over the long term, and engages with policymakers and other stakeholders through entities we've created, including the GC Institute and Health Assurance Foundation.

All of this allows General Catalyst to attack some of the world's hardest problems, including healthcare, climate change, responsible AI, and next-generation national defense. Our healthcare effort is the furthest along, and it maps to our principles. The effort began as an accident. But such accidents (or luck) are why we have the principle *Serendipity must become intentional.* In 2005, while still in Boston, I got a call from Partners Healthcare asking if we could help them figure out what to do with their electronic medical records, or EMRs. My first question was, "What's an EMR?" I had to hire a physician to help me read and understand them.

The Transformation Principles

That's how I began to learn about what was broken in healthcare and how unhelpful technology had been to the industry. That in turn led me to cofound Humedica, which I mentioned earlier did not succeed because it did not adequately collaborate with the existing system. I learned our collaboration principle the hard way.

But the serendipity of getting that call to work on a healthcare problem turned into the intentionality of wanting our company to play a role in transforming healthcare. General Catalyst started Livongo and learned more from that experience. We started Commure so that new healthcare technologies could have a single platform to build on. We started our partnerships with health systems so we could collaborate with incumbents. We wrote the book *UnHealthcare* to map out a future we were determined to create. We took the outrageous step—for a VC company—of buying a health system in Ohio. The result is that now, instead of just funding health tech companies and hoping for the best, we've nurtured an entire movement among health systems and tech companies to reinvent the way we take care of our bodies and minds, ultimately making healthcare more affordable, equitable, and proactive. We continue to invest in startups that are taking the risk of building new technology that can help transform traditional "sick care" into "health assurance." To help the sector test, adopt, and use these technologies to transform care, we work with our coalition of hospital systems. Tech companies can work with and learn from the best incumbent healthcare systems and vice versa.

General Catalyst's healthcare push has taught us how we can approach transformation in other sectors, such as climate and defense. Of course, our company exists to generate returns, and we have done well in that regard. I can't emphasize enough that we

The Case for the Transformation Principles

are capitalists. By generating high returns, we prove our point about transformation principles and get permission—and more capital—to keep investing that way. Our approach and our success have brought us amazing talent. As our flywheel turns, we have ever more capital to invest in big problems—and more brainpower to make sure our portfolio companies thrive.

I want our transformation principles to influence venture capital investors and every kind of investor so they, too, contribute to powerful positive change and steer us away from unintended consequences and toward inclusive capitalism. I want founders to build principle-led companies that thrive for a century, solve great problems, and adroitly navigate changing times.

CHAPTER ONE

THE BUSINESS MUST HAVE A SOUL

I n my work as a venture capitalist, I look at about 1,000 companies a year. Of those, I typically invest in five. What is it about the companies that I say yes to? The answer is multilayered, but it starts with this principle: *The business must have a soul.*

Venture capital typically works like this: A large number of companies come to us from many different sources. Some are introduced to our company by people in our network—could be friends, or founders we've funded in the past, or other VCs, or any number of connections. Startup founders also reach out to us cold, most likely by email. Many companies we pretty quickly decide aren't right for General Catalyst, and we turn them down. The promising companies may be invited to meet with us in our offices or on video if we can't make personal meetings work. We ultimately decide many of those aren't right for us either. But a fraction of those companies get us excited. When that happens, we put together a term sheet—a document that says how much we'll invest and what valuation we would give the company (which determines how much of the equity we'll own). The terms can include other conditions, such as whether we want a seat on the

The Transformation Principles

board. The best companies typically get competing offers from a few VCs, so they consider the term sheet and what else the VC might bring to the table—like a reputation for being a helpful advisor or a success rate in that company's market sector. Sometimes, a company will decide to turn *us* down at that point and go with another VC. But if everyone involved is happy and wants to do the deal, we all sign the term sheet, General Catalyst invests, and the company joins our portfolio.

And then . . . only a few of the companies in our portfolio turn into breakout successes. We, like every startup investor, get it wrong way more than we get it right. But the few that we get right generate massive, enduring returns. That's the nature of venture capital.

So, then, back to the earlier question: Why do a select few companies make the cut? Why do we believe those at least have a chance of breakout success?

The business idea itself has to be interesting, of course. But what matters more is the answer to one of the first questions I'll ask a founder: Why did you start this company?

I can illustrate how that question and the principle about soul informs investment decisions with the story of Mukesh Chatter, CEO and cofounder of Alsym Energy, which is developing a completely new kind of battery—a departure from the battery technologies we know—to both empower the world's poorest people and help ease climate change.

Back in the 1990s, Mukesh founded Nexabit Networks, which built switches that could carry data and video along with phone calls. In 1999, Lucent bought Nexabit for about $900 million. Mukesh took his windfall and invested in startups for about a decade . . . until his mother was diagnosed with late-stage ovarian cancer. Mukesh dove into trying to save her, pouring money into every possible treatment. It extended her life by only a little beyond what the doctors had projected. "I realized no amount of money could save her life," Mukesh says now. "And then I wondered, why am I on this treadmill of making more money if it made no difference in saving my loved one's life? My wife and I said to ourselves that we will not do anything anymore that's not for the larger good."[5]

They decided that they would not look for a billion-*dollar* problem to solve, like most founders and investors—they would, instead, seek out a billion-*person* problem to solve. This would be a company, not a nonprofit. Mukesh believed in capitalism as a way to solve big problems. So it had to be a good business, generating cash flow to operate and grow, but it also had to be a business that would help a billion people live better lives. Mukesh felt this mission deep in his soul.

After some exploration, Mukesh landed on the problem. About two billion people have electricity from the grid only part-time or not at all. Those two billion people, as Mukesh says, are living like it's the nineteenth century. They don't have lights, so school-age kids can't read and study. They get left behind in a world of internet connectedness. They make no economic progress. And existing batteries are not a solution. Common household batteries don't provide enough power. Lead-acid batteries fail after 9 to 12 months. Lithium-ion batteries cost too much and tend to go up in flames.

To tackle this problem, Mukesh set a goal to develop a battery that could cost very little, be extremely safe, and power at least two lightbulbs, one fan, one small refrigerator, and one internet connection. When he took those specs to battery specialists, most

The Transformation Principles

told him he was nuts—it couldn't be done. "Everyone told us it was a moon shot," Mukesh says. (Another example of a beginner's mind at work!) But then he found Nikhil Koratkar, a professor at Rensselaer Polytechnic Institute (RPI); Rahul Mukherjee, a researcher at RPI; and Kripa Varanasi, a professor at MIT. All specialized in some aspect of battery technology, and all were up for the challenge. They together cofounded Alsym Energy in 2015 and started work on new battery technology. They had a working model by 2022, refined it further through 2024, and started shipping samples in early 2025. While Mukesh is guarded about the battery's details, he's told journalists that one electrode is primarily manganese oxide, an abundant mineral that's already produced in mass quantities, while a second is primarily a widely available transition metal oxide. The electrolyte is primarily water based instead of the flammable organic solvents used in lithium-ion batteries (the kind of batteries that power electric cars and e-bikes), which makes the Alsym batteries safer.

As you might expect, Mukesh was already wealthy by the time he built Alsym. He didn't have to work hard—or work at all. But his story told me that he felt Alsym's mission in his soul, which in turn gave the company a soul. When a company has a meaningful soul, its founders and employees will run through walls to achieve the goal. They won't give up. An electrical engineer by training, Mukesh read hundreds of papers on battery technology and worked alongside his scientists. "I've wondered sometimes why I work like a dog," he says, "but if I can light up those homes..."

I first met Mukesh when I was still a new associate at General Catalyst, working in Boston. We were both born in India and occasionally met at Indian social events. By the time he was looking to raise money to scale Alsym, I was in the Bay Area running the company. He came to my home and told me his story. I understood his mission and felt how deeply it meant to him and knew I wanted to invest.

In the meantime, Alsym's technology is proving to have many more applications than Mukesh once thought feasible. Its batteries have the capacity to do much more than light up homes or support utility grids. They will become powerful enough and safe enough to power whole factories. "You can't put lithium-ion batteries next to a steel plant—they'd blow up!" Mukesh says.* But now there is a potential future where a steel plant or other metal processing plant or chemical plants could operate on batteries, cutting enormous amounts of carbon emissions. Alsym could power data centers, military field hospitals, disaster zone operations, and mines. "We have a chance now to make an even much bigger difference than we thought," he says.

While I don't know how the Alsym mission will ultimately turn out, it was important to me that it started with an authentic story. I'd rather invest in someone like that than a cool technology that has no authentic purpose.

Finally, because Mukesh and founders like him are on missions that come from their souls, they are likely to build and run their companies until the mission is complete. They are not in business to exit and go buy a yacht. They're in it to solve the problems that matter to them.

---

* Even small lithium-ion batteries, such as those that power electric bikes, have a tendency to catch fire. Some have caused houses or apartment buildings to burn down. Imagine the damage possible if a whole block of lithium-ion batteries were attached to a factory full of 2,500-degree Farenheit steel smelters.

The Transformation Principles

The company I founded before joining General Catalyst didn't have a soul. I started it because of FOMO—fear of missing out. The mobile phone sector was taking flight, and I didn't want to be left behind. So I started a mobile phone software company for the sake of starting a mobile phone software company. Without a soul or a true north that came from a life story, we crumpled once adversity hit us.

In my first years at General Catalyst, some of the companies we funded or incubated similarly didn't have a real foundational story. I started to see a pattern. The companies lacking soul also tended to lack impact and endurance. The founders who started a company to change or fix something that mattered to their lives had better odds of long-term success. For us as investors, backing companies with a soul led to greater odds of long-term compounding returns. "Soul" surfaced as a key indicator of long-term thinking and enduring positive impact. And by now, years later, I've realized that soul activates all the other principles in this book. It is the one ingredient that connects all of the principles.

But what does that mean—soul? It's become almost cliché for VC firms to say, "We back mission-driven founders." There's certainly nothing wrong with that. No one should back a founder who is starting a company because they don't know what else to do in life—or, like me in my younger days, because they don't want to miss out on a trend. But "mission" is too shallow. Someone can be on a soulless mission to make a billion dollars or a destructive mission to make untraceable 3D-printed guns. Soul is deeper, more meaningful, and directed at powerful, positive change. It comes from a founder's life story, permeates the company's culture, and

The Business Must Have a Soul

acts like a magnet attracting talented people who believe in the founder's goals. When founders imbue their companies with soul, that soul tends to live on long after the founder departs. Soulless companies might have employees, customers, and partners. Soulful companies create followers and movements.

In past decades, technology was typically deployed to make something that we already did (like manufacture products, care for patients, distribute content, and so on) more efficient. It was the essence of automation. But we're now amid an AI-driven tech explosion that is allowing us to *reinvent* the way we do things—especially big, important things. We can reinvent education and healthcare and energy and transportation. It's this reinvention that requires much more than a mission if we're going to get it right. It needs a soul and a deep sense of meaning and a desire to fix what's broken.

This is not a new idea. Many of the great companies in history were founded with a soul, and in most cases that soul lived on in the culture for decades after the founder left the scene. Steve Jobs at Apple had an all-consuming belief in design and in making computing easy "for the rest of us." Years after Jobs passed, the company still has that dedication. Phil Knight at Nike was devoted to getting us all to be active, not just to selling shoes. I've heard it said that he's done more to prevent heart disease than all the cardiologists put together. Knight's soul-driven mission has guided Nike throughout its 60-year history. Walt Disney's very being continues to be the heart and soul of the company he founded in 1923.

When a startup founder approaches General Catalyst, how do we know if that person and that company have a soul? It really does begin with asking why the founder started the company. If

The Transformation Principles

someone comes in with a pitch deck, I usually tell them to put it aside. If they're coming in with a lived experience, they don't need a deck. I just want to hear their story. As that story unfolds, it's not hard to see whether it is authentic or manufactured. You can sense the passion and sincerity—the kind I heard from Mukesh. I need to feel that the company is the founder's life's work—that the founder's greatest desire is to spend decades guiding a company that has a meaningful impact.

This, too, is where a beginner's mind—for me!—becomes important. When I listen to the stories behind the companies, I don't listen with an expert's mind, thinking that I know what can or can't be done. No investor can know as much as someone who comes in with a deeply lived experience that is driving their passion for building a company. When I listened to Mukesh's story, I came to believe that whether his idea would make money was not the most important thing. Instead, I believed he was determined to use technology to fix inequalities in the world and reduce climate change, and that he would learn and maneuver until he found a way to do that. Where my expertise came into play is that in order to fund him, I only had to believe that the problem he was setting out to solve was big and important enough, and that if I was going to bet on anyone to solve it, it would be him. In short, I had to believe he had a soul that drove him to do this, and that his soul was pointed at the right problem.

Not all of our portfolio companies have an origin story as emotional as Mukesh's, but a lot do.

Qasar Younis's story was instrumental in convincing General Catalyst to invest in a category that we otherwise might have thought was overhyped and overcrowded: self-driving cars.

Qasar was practically raised in the auto industry. He came

The Business Must Have a Soul

to the United States from Pakistan, sponsored by an uncle who worked for General Motors, and then lived just outside the GM Technical Center in Warren, Michigan. He attended the General Motors Institute of Technology, now known as Kettering University, and worked at General Motors and then Bosch (the leading parts supplier in automotive) before joining Google in the early 2010s. At Google, Qasar was exposed to the company's work on self-driving cars, and he had two competing thoughts: First, the technology was still too early; second, it was going to eventually happen, and at that point the car would shift from being a hardware-defined product to a software-defined one. Having been steeped in the Midwest auto industry experience, Qasar believed that Silicon Valley's boast that it was going to "disrupt" cars was misplaced. The car was going to be reinvented by the players who knew cars—the people at GM, Ford, Fiat Chrysler, and global auto companies like Volkswagen and Toyota—and this reinvention was going to be an *evolution*, not a revolution. He teamed with his friend Peter Ludwig—Qasar and Peter worked together at Google and found that their parents lived a quarter mile from each other in Michigan—and founded Applied Intuition. The company's mission is to build software tools to sell to the automakers to help them build the AI that will make cars increasingly software driven.[6]

If I had relied on Silicon Valley's accepted wisdom, I probably would've never met with Applied Intuition. But Qasar's story—his soul—told me that he saw what others didn't, and that his devotion to the auto industry and to helping it reinvent transportation meant he would plow through every hurdle in his way. As of this writing, 18 of the top 20 automakers are customers of Applied Intuition.

The Transformation Principles

One of the most important initiatives at General Catalyst has been to transform the broken, frustrating, expensive traditional healthcare system into a new system of what we call health assurance. In a health assurance system, AI can help medical professionals deeply understand the health of every individual and proactively help each of us stay well and out of the old system of doctor visits and hospital stays. If we as a society are going to take on something as big and challenging as reinventing healthcare, we need soul-driven companies to see it through. And we've found many.

In the first conversation I had with Toyin Ajayi, as usual I asked about the origin story of the company she'd cofounded, Cityblock Health. The company had been spun out of Google's Sidewalk Labs in 2016 and was looking for funding, but I wanted to know what happened before Google. Toyin was a physician, and when she had gone to work inside hospital systems, she saw how badly those systems were failing low-income, marginalized people. "I realized I'd find it hard to have the kind of career I wanted inside the system," she says. "I needed to be part of something that took care of people differently."[7] What that was, she didn't know. She quit and went to work for a healthcare nonprofit in Massachusetts. She went to protests. "I carried a placard in my trunk that said, 'Healthcare is a human right!'" she notes. "I was looking for a way to live my values. The nonprofit work couldn't scale. Americans have collectively chosen capitalism as a mechanism for doing things. So I decided to try that. If I build a good business getting healthcare to poor people, if it's scalable and profitable, people who might not normally invest will do so, because it's a good business."

She and another healthcare veteran, Iyah Romm, started

The Business Must Have a Soul

working on ideas. In 2016, Google heard about her work and asked her to join as an entrepreneur in residence. She and Romm built Cityblock inside Sidewalk Labs. Cityblock is basically betting that it can use technology paired with high-touch clinical expertise to find and care for marginalized patients in a way that costs less than traditional healthcare—because with traditional healthcare, low-income, uninsured people often show up at a hospital emergency room only when they're very sick, and that costs insurers like Medicaid a fortune. So Cityblock partners with payers in a value-based contract, taking a lump sum of what a patient's healthcare would normally cost—as much as $20,000 annually—and then taking responsibility for that patient's care. If Cityblock keeps the patient healthy while holding down the cost of that patient's care to, say, $10,000, the company keeps the money it saves and shares some with the insurer.

Toyin's lived experience led to her cofounding Cityblock. She is doing what her soul told her to do. And her soul is pointed at a problem that is enormous—the United States spent $872 billion on Medicaid in 2023.[8] And it's a problem that if solved would be an enormous benefit to society, keeping more people healthy and out of hospitals. Toyin believed that working within the constraints of capitalism and collaborating with nonprofits and government programs was the way to create a sustainable solution to the problem, so I knew her soul would not let her quit until she found a formula that would work as a viable business.

Cityblock is not a mainstream kind of Silicon Valley investment—in fact, as Toyin recalled, Google (or, now, Alphabet) spun it out because it basically didn't know what to make of the company. But Toyin's story added up to a reason for us to believe in her.

The Transformation Principles

The concept that a soul has to be genuine yet also has to be pointed at the right problem is important. Although this principle almost made me miss one of the best investments General Catalyst has made.

The first time Zach Reitano came into our office to tell us about the company he cofounded, then called Roman, he told us his story, and we could see the soul inside his business. In his twenties, Zach discovered that he had a heart condition that led to erectile dysfunction—an existential crisis for a man at that age. His father was a physician, so Zach had no trouble getting a diagnosis and a prescription for ED medication. But he realized he was lucky—for most men, getting ED meds can be difficult, embarrassing, and expensive. Pfizer's Viagra was about to come off patent, which meant generic sildenafil would be available much more cheaply. Zach was setting up a business that would let men with ED get diagnosed via telemedicine in the privacy of their homes, get a prescription, and have authentic medication sent directly to them. It was apparent that Zach felt he was on a mission to help men with ED. But in his first pass with us, Roman seemed to me more like a straightforward e-commerce company, selling a product online. While General Catalyst did invest in Roman early on, I didn't get involved because I thought the opportunity for impact on healthcare was too small.

In reality, Zach and his cofounders, Saman Rahmanian and Rob Schutz, had a much more impactful idea in mind—an idea several levels up from just helping people with ED. Zach's father had saved him from his condition, and in fact at other times he had saved the lives of both his mother and sister too. That happened because his father lived with them, and, as a doctor, he intimately knew about their health, which allowed him to intervene proactively when he detected something was wrong. What Zach actually wanted to do with his company was, in his words, "Re-create my dad in software."[9] He wryly added: "I'm sure therapists would have a lot to say about that!" ED was just a starting point. Zach came back to me to show how he wanted to build out from the ED business in ways that would allow Roman—now called Ro—to create relationships with patients, gather data, and help those patients improve their health through software in the way his father might've done in real life in his household. If it all goes as planned, Ro's goal is to scale high-quality, chronic care. Once I understood that, I believed that Zach deeply felt a need to reinvent healthcare so everyone would have the benefit he got from his father. He was imbuing Ro with his soul, and it was pointed at reinventing healthcare. I was wrong at first and didn't see what Zach intended me to see, but once it clicked that he was building a company with a soul pointed at a huge problem, I went all in.

In my early years of running General Catalyst, our founders in the Boston area were passionate about investing in good people who were running good companies. We were pretty typical VCs, and we became a solid, successful company.

Once I took the reins, I looked to Ken Chenault, the former Amex CEO, as a mentor. I wanted to learn how American Express morphed through so many stages yet was always the same company at its core. That's what I wanted for General Catalyst, 18 years after its founding—to establish an entity that would go through many leaders after me, tune itself to the times, and have

The Transformation Principles

societal impact with innovation for generations. Ken pushed me to understand my soul and better articulate it so that it could flow into General Catalyst. And true to what I've shared in this chapter, that soul could only come from my authentic lived experience—my spirituality, my dedication to responsible innovation, and my belief in relying on capitalism to reinvent industries and fix problems in ways that make society more equitable and inclusive; all of that comes from how my life has unfolded. The principles in this book are a way of codifying what's in my soul and the company's soul so that anyone else can understand why we exist and how we work.

As described earlier, building on the foundation of our soul and these principles, our company is on a mission to transform the way we take care of our health. As noted, early on I invested in and/or helped start a handful of health tech companies, like Humedica and Livongo. Those investments led to my understanding of how broken and misaligned our healthcare system is. Another investment I made was in Color Health, which started out by developing software that can analyze our DNA. I joined Color's board, and during one board meeting, we got into a discussion about how to get consumers to engage with DNA testing. Most of Color's customers were doing it out of curiosity. But we knew that DNA testing is a foundation for long-term proactive healthcare. It can flag potential future health problems and give an individual a chance to head them off. But humans aren't programmed to think long-term. They need to be incentivized to do that. In the meeting, someone brought up the similarity to saving money for retirement, and how the creation of 401(k) plans incentivized that by making your contributions tax-deferred. I realized that the whole healthcare system does very little to incentivize long-term thinking about your health. The whole system is built around—and makes its money from—treating you only after you get sick. It is a massive misalignment with what's best for people. What we really want is to *not* get sick in the first place. If our soul at GC is about activating founders, innovators, and others in our ecosystem to transform industries and create positive impact plus returns, then we could have a massive positive impact by changing the nature of healthcare to what we call "health assurance." We feel it is the right—and most urgent—initial application of our soul for this moment in time. And because we approach this mission with a goal of creating an enduring, positive societal impact, great leaders like Ken Chenault and Merck's former CEO Ken Frazier have opted to join us and guide us on this journey.

However, as important as "the business must have a soul" is, it's also not enough. That's why there are nine principles. As you'll see, I look at companies through the lens of all of the principles. Few companies come into our offices satisfying every one of them. But each principle is involved in guiding how we think about who we want to work with for the long haul.

CHAPTER TWO

NAVIGATING AMBIGUITY IS MORE VALUABLE THAN PREDICTING THE FUTURE

There is a future that I want General Catalyst to help create. It's a future where inclusive capitalism prioritizes impact plus returns and is a mechanism for enduring positive outcomes. That future is our North Star.

Yet I don't know how to get there. And that's the way it should be.

As we reinvent our company and label what we're doing "venture beyond," what we know is that the "beyond" is a transformation company, the first of its kind. We don't have some prescribed template we are trying to replicate. But we know we're generally headed to our true north, and I'm comfortable with that ambiguity, as long as we keep activating the most ambitious talent and let our soul guide us in our quest to build a better world with inclusive capitalism.

Our company knows that the route to the future we seek will be winding and unpredictable. It will depend on countless factors such as advancements in technology, changes in the political climate, shifts in the global economic ecosystem, and public

The Transformation Principles

opinion. We may at times go the wrong way or stall, and at other times we might catch favorable winds and race along faster than expected. But successfully navigating such ambiguity is what is valuable—more valuable than making a prediction about the future and "knowing" how to get there.

If General Catalyst is determined to race straight toward our believed-in future in spite of what we encounter along the way, we'll likely fail before we get halfway to our destination. And then we'll have failed to learn from and take advantage of unexpected twists and turns. It's like the story of American explorers Lewis and Clark: Their goal was to open a way for the United States to expand to the West Coast, but what they learned about the terrain and people and wildlife on their journey was more valuable than finding a route to the sea.

The points we've already discussed in this book are key to successfully navigating ambiguity toward the future. The company must have a soul, because companies with a soul have the resilience and drive to find their way through murky times. The leadership team must confront ambiguity with a beginner's mind, unimpeded by conventional wisdom that can throw up obstacles, so the team can instead imagine what could be. And the beginner's mind needs to be grounded in a set of principles—principles that help leaders make the right decisions amid the fog of uncertainty.

Ironically, I often get credit for accurately predicting the future because General Catalyst invests in non-obvious company ideas that don't seem to fit any pattern, and many of those companies end up creating a future most didn't anticipate. But this happens because I *don't* pretend to know the future. I can see the big problems to solve today, and I know that if a particular company

Navigating Ambiguity Is More Valuable

solves one, that company has a good chance of becoming a significant success. But I don't predict exactly what that solution and future will be like and push for the company to produce it. The future doesn't unfold that way. Instead, I look for a founder or company that has a soul pointed at a big problem, and I look for the intelligence and passion and beginner's mind that will help the company steer through ambiguity, always watching for new directions and opportunities that will help bring about the believed-in future—or an even better future that no one could have imagined.

I've been learning about this principle over and over throughout my life. It started when I was a student at MIT. I didn't go in with an idea about what I wanted to be when I grew up—like, *Oh, I want to be a great academic at MIT*—and work backward to plot a path to get there. Instead, I followed my curiosity and learned to be a lifelong learner, which would help me gain the capability to navigate ambiguity. I didn't fully realize what I was doing at the time, but when I look back, after college that mindset allowed me to zigzag through cofounding a company, through my early years as a venture capitalist, through leading General Catalyst, and, now, through working to reinvent healthcare, energy, and other big sectors.

Even now, I get reminded about the value of navigating ambiguity to solve a big societal problem. When I cofounded Livongo with Glen Tullman, we only knew that diabetes was an enormous problem that had mostly bad solutions. We didn't—couldn't—predict what the right solution would be, but we knew that if we applied technology and creative thinking, we would eventually find a great solution. Glen had the soul I was looking for. He'd already been CEO of a healthcare tech company, Allscripts, taking

The Transformation Principles

it public at a two-billion-dollar valuation. He and I both invested in medical-data company Humedica. So he knew and cared about healthcare. He also has a son and mother who have diabetes, so he intimately knows that the healthcare system is bad at helping people who have diabetes manage their condition so they can live a reasonably carefree life. Livongo was launched in 2014 with a soul, an important purpose, and a beginner's mentality. At first, we experimented and hit dead ends. Over time, a new future started to take shape. We could give a patient a smart glucometer that would feed data about that person's blood sugar, medical condition, activities, lifestyle, and eating habits to artificial intelligence software. The software, backed up by human medical professionals, would come to understand each individual's diabetes and guide each patient like a guardian angel, working to keep the condition at bay.

The future isn't about having people with diabetes see more doctors and get more tests. It's about helping each person manage the condition so they see as little as possible of doctors and get fewer tests. By navigating ambiguity, a better future than we'd imagined appeared. The digital health sector came to believe in that future, too, and Teladoc Health bought Livongo for $18 billion.

By the way, Livongo's outcome showed me another lesson about navigating ambiguity. We started Livongo to change the healthcare experience for patients. We thought we could get to a better future by starting companies that would disrupt an old way of doing things. But trying to change something as complex, enormous, and entrenched as healthcare from the outside doesn't work. When we sold Livongo, it was treating about 500,000 diabetic patients. There are more than 30

Navigating Ambiguity Is More Valuable

million people with diabetes in the United States alone. While in certain ways Livongo was a huge success, it fell far short of General Catalyst's long-term goal of reinventing the healthcare experience. But we learned a lesson, and after selling Livongo our company decided to pursue an unconventional strategy for reinventing healthcare: We'd partner with major healthcare incumbents, buy a hospital system, and together *with the system* invent products and services that will change the healthcare experience. No venture firm had ever done anything like it. But by navigating through the ambiguity, we saw a different path that could lead us to our desired future. (The process also led us to fully embrace the seventh principle in this book: *For great change, radical collaboration beats disruption.* I'll explain more about that principle later.)

Navigating ambiguity with a beginner's mind took us to a different future than we had imagined. The future didn't dictate our path; instead, the path created the future.

Beyond healthcare, General Catalyst is creating a movement to change the nature of capitalism—to create a future where inclusive capitalism prioritizes impact plus returns and is a mechanism for enduring positive outcomes. Exactly what does that future look like? I don't know. I only know that we have to get there, and that the path will be bumpy and unpredictable. We will have to navigate with a beginner's mind and with our first principles as a foundation.

As the CEO of an investment company, do I know for sure that we'll get the best returns operating this way? No. But I believe we will in the long run. And by believing that in my soul, it becomes contagious. Others in the organization buy into it. Highly respected people like Ken Chenault and Ken Frazier come

The Transformation Principles

to believe it, too, and want to be a part of it. We're on a journey of discovery. Our bet is that such a journey will help us get to the right future, and our investments along the way will result in enduring returns and positive impact.

History is littered with companies that predicted a future that wasn't quite right and hurried to build their vision too soon. Sometimes, such companies describe a future so compelling that very smart people get drawn in and invest a lot of money in the enterprise. It's almost always a mistake.

One well-known example is General Magic, the subject of a 2018 documentary (also called *General Magic*).* The company was started as a project inside Apple and was spun out in 1990, several years before the beginning of the consumer internet era. General Magic's founders—Marc Porat, Andy Hertzfeld, and Bill Atkinson—had been important contributors to Apple's early success. They had a vision of a future where devices would be connected to a global network in a digital alternate reality where people could work, shop, and socialize. The company set out to build every aspect of this system themselves—the devices, the software, and the cartoonish black-and-white digital world we'd experience. The team imagined a virtual space that you'd navigate by "walking" down a virtual street and going into graphical depictions of doors that might lead into a store or library or office. General Magic's pitch stirred a lot of excitement. Huge corporations

---

* As a journalist at *USA Today* in the 1990s, Kevin Maney visited General Magic and often wrote about the company.

Navigating Ambiguity Is More Valuable

including Sony, Motorola, Philips, and AT&T became investors or partners. But while the General Magic team was right broadly about the future, it was wrong specifically. Yes, we'd end up with digital devices connected to a network, but not in the way General Magic foretold. By 1994, companies such as Yahoo, Netscape, and Amazon had started building pieces of the internet that looked nothing like what General Magic imagined—and more like what it actually became. Instead of seeing what was emerging and navigating through those times and learning, General Magic stuck to its version of the future. By 1999, just as the dot-com boom peaked and the world was in an internet-crazy frenzy, General Magic was out of sync with the industry and started falling apart. In 2002, the company shut down.

Another company, Linden Lab, founded in 1999, believed in a future of virtual worlds, something like what we now refer to as the metaverse.[10] Visitors to its world, Second Life, would be avatars, and the virtual world would have its own economy—concepts that are more familiar now. But, again, Linden Lab's vision of the future was correct broadly and wrong specifically. Instead of learning and navigating, it stuck too close to its vision. It could have become the company that everyone associates with the emerging metaverse, but it's a company that most people have probably never heard of.

In contrast are companies that foresaw a future broadly but understood that the specifics would emerge over time. It's not a coincidence that these are the companies we know and rely on today.

An example is Netflix, founded in 1997. From the start, CEO Reed Hastings and his leadership team foresaw a future where consumers would watch digital movies that streamed in over the

The Transformation Principles

internet. But in 1997, the internet wasn't ready for that. Most people were still dialing in through superslow modems over phone lines. So, Netflix began its business by letting users go on its website to order movies to rent, and the movies would arrive through the mail on DVDs. For the next 10 years, Netflix observed the unfolding of the internet and devices that connect to it, adjusting its plans and looking for the right moment to bring the future alive—all the while sticking to its DVD service even as other companies prematurely launched streaming services that were clunky and unreliable. When Netflix finally launched streaming in 2007, it had gotten the future right. Netflix had landed on a future that the Netflix of 1997 couldn't have fully imagined. And, by the way, the Netflix of today is also one of the most successful producers of movies and TV shows—a result of continuing to navigate changing times. As the popularity of streaming grew in the 2000s, movie rights holders increasingly wouldn't sell many of the top films to Netflix. The company responded by ramping up its own productions. In 2023, Netflix won six Academy Awards out of its 16 nominations.[11] By navigating ambiguity toward a broad concept of the future, Netflix wound up with a kind of triumph that certainly wasn't in a future anyone could have predicted in 1997.

As an investor, when I encounter a company that has a passionate soul pointed at a significant problem, the next thing I want to know is whether the company's leaders have the ability to navigate ambiguity with a beginner's mind. "Experts" who have a very

Navigating Ambiguity Is More Valuable

specific future mapped out might succeed in the long run, but the odds will be against them. I would rather get behind people like Mukesh at Alsym and Zach at Ro—founders who broadly see a desired future but will get there one discovery and decision at a time.

Mukesh wants to create a future that gives two billion people a better chance in life and marches us toward stopping destructive climate change. Right now, the mechanism to do that is a new kind of battery. I'm convinced that if technology or other conditions change and Mukesh sees better ways to achieve his mission, he will adapt, because he is not tied to a specific version of the future.

Zach wants a future where everyone has access to personalized, goal-oriented medical care online. Zach is in sync with this chapter's principle in his approach to the future. "We knew where we wanted to start, and what would provide immediate value to customers," Zach told me.[12] As noted earlier, Ro started with erectile dysfunction medicine—in a way, Ro's version of Netflix's DVDs. It was a straightforward offering that was possible to pull off right away. "We also know our North Star," Zach added, "but we don't exactly know how to get there." When the COVID-19 pandemic raced through the United States in 2020, Ro saw an opportunity to move toward its future amid this unforeseeable event. Ro worked with health officials to set up an in-home vaccination program for the elderly or homebound. It directionally fit with Ro's goal of using technology to make healthcare accessible and easy, and it helped the company gain more users and more attention. If Ro's team had been laser focused on "build my dad in software," it likely wouldn't have made the decision to get into

The Transformation Principles

COVID-19 vaccinations, or later broaden its offering to dermatology, fertility, and weight loss.

Inside Ro, Zach uses an interesting analogy to promote the concept of navigating ambiguity toward the future. "I tell my team to embrace their inner camel," he says. Camels are built to withstand harsh conditions for long periods of time. They adapt and keep moving toward their destination. If a sandstorm blows in, they have nostrils that can close to keep sand out and hooves that splay so they don't slide on a dune. When there's no water, they can go without any for days and then rehydrate faster than any mammal. Whatever happens, they adapt to conditions and don't stop. "The ability to adapt is so important because people can't predict the future, or they can't predict it on the right time horizon," says Zach. Ro now offers a range of healthcare products and services for men and women and is one of the best-known online healthcare companies in the United States.

The story of another General Catalyst portfolio company, Samsara, is a terrific example of how navigating ambiguity works in action. Sanjit Biswas and John Bicket had previously founded a cloud networking company called Meraki that they sold to Cisco for $1.2 billion in 2012. That gave them money to start something else, and there was a problem in the world that was bothering them: Physical goods companies, like a soft drink bottler or a lawn mower maker, were often being left out of the digital revolution. "Meraki was essentially the commercialization of our PhD research," Sanjit says. "What we were going to do next, we wanted to be bigger and more impactful. It meant building for the long term, focusing on an underserved market. It was a massive problem space and opportunity for impact."[13]

Navigating Ambiguity Is More Valuable

As Sanjit told me, pieces of technology that could help such companies, like wireless digital sensors that could connect to the cloud, were available, but they weren't really being assembled into solutions that could meaningfully help those companies. Sometime in the future, if cloud-connected sensors were everywhere, any company should be able to have a real-time digital copy of its physical operations, and the digital copy could be analyzed to make the business better. "If you're in construction, for instance, you'd be able to see if you are using all your equipment, whether you should rent some out, or move something to a different location where it's going to be needed," Sanjit says. "In construction, that can make a big difference."

Such a future is a big idea, but where would Samsara start and how would it get there? Sanjit and his team didn't know. "Our original idea was the simplest sensor we could think of—a cloud-connected temperature sensor," Sanjit says. "We cobbled them together from parts we got at Radio Shack and Walgreens." The Samsara team thought commercial beverage makers would want to put them in their refrigeration units, so the sensors could issue an alert if temperatures started rising. "But, we found out that commercial refrigeration units don't break much at all. We heard crickets. Customers weren't into it. But some asked if it was okay if they moved the sensors around. They took them out of the refrigerators and put them into refrigerated vans and trucks that delivered products." Delivery was the weak link. A driver might leave a van door open and products would spoil. "We wouldn't have figured that application out," Sanjit says. "Our customers told us." And Samsara adjusted. One company, artisanal cheese maker Cowgirl Creamery, signed up because it was losing $10,000 worth of cheese a day, usually when delivery vehicle doors got left open

The Transformation Principles

too long. Samsara's sensors can let Cowgirl know where trucks are and monitor the temperatures inside them, sending alerts before anything spoils so managers can, for example, call the driver's cell and say, "Close the door!" Solving that problem for Cowgirl Creamery led Samsara into building sensors and systems to track commercial fleets of all kinds.

"One key is to experiment quickly," Sanjit told me. "Over a weekend we'd write software and buy GPS trackers on Amazon. It was rapid iteration and listening for resonant fit. We'd try other experiments in parallel, like building an energy monitor. Customers didn't know what to do with it—energy monitoring wasn't as important as losing ten thousand dollars of cheese every day. We kept looking for whether customers were asking for more. Then we'd know we were solving the right problem. When we know we're onto something, everyone in the company feels it."

Once Samsara locked in on fleet management as the entryway to the future it imagined, the business got traction and the technology bloomed. It created a category it calls "connected operations cloud." The business expanded beyond trucks and travel and now sells sensors and systems for tracking supply chains, warehousing, construction sites, and other markets. In 2018, Samsara moved into video-based safety products. Dual-facing cameras in the driver's cab can provide real-time video monitored by AI to detect risky behavior such as distracted driving. Whatever the use case, Samsara's sensors send data to AI-driven software that learns about the physical operations and surfaces ways to make them more efficient or safer. Samsara is on a path to allowing any enterprise with physical operations to have a digital duplicate that

Navigating Ambiguity Is More Valuable

AI can analyze. But true to the principle of navigating ambiguity, it didn't get there the way it thought it would, and the details of the future it is creating are different from the ones Sanjit and his team originally envisioned.

"I think if we had tried this ten or twenty years ago, it wouldn't have worked," Sanjit says. "You'd have to educate people how to use an app. The technology wasn't there. Imagine going to the food and beverage industry ten or fifteen years ago and saying, 'Hey, let's do all of your operations digitally.' That would have been a big lift, but now it's kind of obvious."

In 2021, Samsara went public and was worth more than $12 billion. By 2024, its annual recurring revenues were more than $1 billion and growing nearly 40% year over year, and the company had more than 20,000 customers.

When a company founder meets with me about investing, the opening question I usually ask is, "Why did you start this company?" As discussed in the previous chapter, I want to hear a story, and I want that story to show me that the founder's soul is deeply devoted to solving a significant problem. But the details of the story also reveal something else: whether that founder can adapt and grow on the way to creating a better future. Adapting and growing while not giving up is the core competency for navigating ambiguity.

This points to a big reason people get investment decisions wrong: They think of the founder and founding idea as fixed. They hear the big vision and assess what the founder knows, and

The Transformation Principles

they make the investment based on that, failing to understand that both will change. In fact, if both don't change, the company will almost surely suffer. The future is blurry, and the road to get there is ambiguous. But if the founder or founding team can adapt and grow, they will navigate that ambiguity. Investors tend to underestimate how much a good founder can grow. Understanding a person's potential plays a huge part in an investment decision. In fact, one of the most satisfying outcomes is when a founder succeeds far beyond their own expectations.

This has been my personal story too. I'm not the same person I was when I started on this journey with General Catalyst. And I could never have imagined, two decades ago, how my future would turn out. When I started at GC, we were investing in software platforms and thought that was our likely future. But then we saw how limiting that was, and that we had the chance to transform industries and change the way innovation gets funded, built, and scaled. We found out that disrupting from outside isn't nearly as effective as transforming in collaboration with existing enterprises. Positive enduring change requires more than a single company—it requires ecosystems of companies. We've navigated through economic ups and downs, political shifts, a pandemic, and the game-changing, transformational arrival of new-generation AI. If, back at the beginning, we had decided on one vision of the future and stuck with it, we'd probably be out of business by now—or at least irrelevant.

To put it all together, I'm looking for these things to line up in a founder: a driven soul pointed at a big enough problem, a better future they hope to create, the humility and curiosity of a beginner's mind, and the ability to adapt and grow so the company

Navigating Ambiguity Is More Valuable

can blow past difficulties and take advantage of victories and opportunities.

I saw that in Mukesh at Alsym, Zach at Ro, and Sanjit at Samsara. The world witnessed it in Reed Hastings at Netflix and in many other founders who navigated through ambiguity to create a new future for us.

CHAPTER THREE

CREATING THE FUTURE BEATS IMPROVING THE PAST

The first company I cofounded started its life burdened by two original sins. The first, as I've described, was that it didn't have a soul. The second was that we lacked imagination about the future. We looked at the mobile explosion as a way to improve the past—so we built software that would port what was already on the internet onto mobile devices. We didn't understand that when everyone is walking around with connected devices (which also have GPS, a camera, and a phone), we could reinvent what we do online and how we do it. Our shortcoming taught me a lesson: Companies that create a new future and take customers on a journey there are far more exciting, impactful, and enduring than companies that iterate on the past.

Businesses, entrepreneurs, and investors throughout history have too often focused on improving the past. In an oft-cited long-ago example, when television made its way into homes in the 1940s, early producers and broadcasters treated it as an improvement on radio—radio with a picture. Many of the first TV shows had been radio shows—*The Lone Ranger*, *The Amos 'n' Andy Show*—and leaned heavily on dialogue. It was a failure to see TV

The Transformation Principles

as a way to reinvent entertainment. When *I Love Lucy* debuted in 1951, it took advantage of the medium and brought in physical comedy meant to be seen, not just heard. That show opened up a new future. Most of the radio-first programs soon disappeared, while Lucille Ball and Desi Arnaz became the first millionaire TV stars. Similarly, the first cars were dubbed horseless carriages because most people saw them as a carriage pulled by an engine, not as a new future ready to happen. When wireless-connected RFID (radio frequency identification) tags were invented in the 1980s, they were typically seen as an improvement on bar codes (known as UPC, or universal product code, symbols)—not as a way to create a new future where companies could track and make digital models of physical operations, as Samsara is doing now.

Just about every new technology gets first interpreted as an improvement on the past, and yet just about every new technology opens new possible futures. Discontinuous ideas move a field forward, so that the future is not just built upon linear improvements from the past. Often there is a break or total paradigm shift that unlocks a new path, and the best founders are the ones that pick up from the current path and move society to the new ones. Those entrepreneurs are the ones I want to back—and the ones everyone should want to invest in or work for. (And, in fact, the best talent does want to work for such companies.)

This principle of *creating the future beats improving the past* is particularly relevant in the 2020s. Never in my career have there been more opportunities to create new futures and reinvent industries. In 2022, ChatGPT and other generative AI systems avalanched into our lives. Nearly every kind of business is likely to be reinvented by someone who believes that applied AI can create a future the rest of us can't yet imagine. As superpowered

Creating the Future Beats Improving the Past

AI is arriving on the scene, at the same time we're developing a number of other foundational technologies that can lead to new futures. CRISPR is allowing us to edit genes, opening up new approaches to everything from the treatment of diseases to food security. Blockchain and crypto may have largely failed to upgrade money—hardly anyone uses it to actually buy things—but the technology will give us ways to reinvent many business sectors, including medical research. (I invested in a company, HealthEx, that's working on this very idea. More on that later.) As I wrote in *Unscaled*, these new foundational technologies, often in combination, give us ways to reinvent the industries that developed during the twentieth century—industries built on previous-era technologies like electricity, internal combustion engines, and telecommunications. Until recently, software and computing were mostly used to improve existing industries, making them more efficient, faster, and cheaper. But merely improving those industries is not that interesting anymore. The technologies of today and tomorrow can transform old industries and create the future. The real discontinuous improvement is not the copilots that dominate AI today but the agents that do the work on their own, without human supervision (though always with human escape hatches). Hippocratic AI, for instance, is developing healthcare agents that can talk to you about your medication or surgery on the phone, and AI agents from a company called Crescendo can often better help customers who call in with a problem than many human call center operators. (More on both companies later in the book.)

In fact, we *need* innovators to create new futures. Climate change, wars, pandemics, societal divides, inequality—these by-products of the previous industrial age are threatening our

The Transformation Principles

survival and seem more threatening than ever. "Ours is clearly an age of upheaval," wrote Jerome Roos, a political economist and historian, in *The New York Times*.[14] "We are ourselves in the midst of a painful transition, a sort of interregnum, as the Italian political theorist Antonio Gramsci famously called it, between an old world that is dying and a new one that is struggling to be born. Such epochal shifts are inevitably fraught with danger. Yet for all their destructive potential, they are also full of possibility."

It's those possibilities—those new futures—that everyone should desire to invest in, support, and bring to life.

How do I know if a company is creating the future and not just improving the past?

In a similar way that I know a company has a soul. It's often in the story. I want to hear a case for why the past needs to be left behind, not just improved or tweaked. (If a presentation leans heavily on making something *faster* or *cheaper*, the product is just improving the past.) I want to hear how new technologies and new thinking can solve problems an old industry caused or has been failing to fix. I want a sense that a beginner's mind is looking at how things are and believing they can be different, not just better. Sometimes I can hear a mission to create a future in the way a company imagines going to market. If Airbnb had wanted to sell its software to hotel companies, it would've been improving the past—not nearly as captivating as creating a whole new category of hospitality. Same with Uber. It could've sold its technology to taxi or "black car" companies to help them improve how they operate. Instead, Uber created a new category of on-demand

Creating the Future Beats Improving the Past

transportation—a future few could've imagined even a few years before Uber was founded.

That doesn't mean that developing technology for incumbent companies is automatically a failure to create a new future. Applied Intuition is selling software tools to existing automakers to help them create a new future of software-defined and autonomous cars and trucks. The ultimate goal of creating a new future is what counts.

Keep in mind, as I wrote in the previous chapter, that I'm not looking for a founder to show me a specific future. I want a founder who sees a better future broadly and is setting out to discover the future that needs to unfold.

Anduril is a good example of how this principle works. When I first met with the founders, they told a story that convinced me that it is critical to create a new future for the US military. The need for that future is why I made a decision—hotly debated inside General Catalyst—to invest in the company.

On the surface, there is a lot about Anduril that would scare off many Silicon Valley VCs. Over the past few decades, venture-backed tech companies have generally avoided making military products, in part because a lot of talented technical people didn't want to work on any kind of weapon or spying technology. (That's been changing since Russia started a war with Ukraine in 2022.) Anduril was cofounded by Palmer Luckey, who started tinkering with VR headsets when he was 16, developed the Oculus Rift headset, and sold his business to Facebook in 2014 for two billion dollars. He had a prickly departure from Facebook in 2016 and publicly supported Donald Trump for president that year. In 2017, Luckey started Anduril with three former executives of Palantir Technologies—Matt Grimm, Trae Stephens, and Brian

The Transformation Principles

Schimpf—and former Oculus product lead Joe Chen. Among Anduril's first projects was an autonomous surveillance system along the US–Mexican border, sometimes referred to as a virtual wall at a time when Trump was driving to build a physical wall there. Add it all up, and as Schimpf, the CEO of Anduril, admits: "When we started, we were quite controversial."[15]

This, I believe, is where a beginner's mentality helped me. I wasn't burdened by having expertise in the defense industry. I didn't know what was possible or not possible. I wanted to hear the founders' story with an open mind. Brian recalls meeting me for lunch to talk about the business. He says that I "quickly honed in on the interesting dimensions and what needed to be true to make this happen. It was less pitch and more relationship building."

The Anduril story I heard from them started this way:

The US defense industry is stuck in the past, building ever more expensive weapons that have ever more limited effectiveness in current and future confrontations. The incumbent defense industry is focused on making big, powerful hardware—fighter jets, ships, missiles, tanks. But software is and will be the key to winning wars and deterring enemies. Anduril's founders told me about a Defense Advanced Research Projects Agency (DARPA) concept called Mosaic Warfare, which describes a future "where ubiquitous and affordable unmanned air and ground platforms find targets on a contested battlefield and pass the information to a decision maker who can instantly task another part of the same system to strike the enemy from safety."

The battlefield of the future, Brian and his cofounders asserted, will be won with unmanned drones and robots, all driven by AI and connected together so they can share information, help each other, and relay data back to human commanders. But

Creating the Future Beats Improving the Past

today's defense companies build hardware and install software to control it—often clunky software that doesn't connect to other military systems. Anduril believes in a different future, where weapons start with the capabilities that software and data can enable, and hardware is built to help the software do its job. To get on a path to that future, Anduril has developed a battlefield operating system, Lattice, that can connect all the different smart military systems, and it offers a few varieties of land, sea, and air drones that can gather and transmit reconnaissance data.

Brian told me that Anduril wants to be the company showing the way to an entirely new defense industry. The founders also argued that software-forward defense is a better deterrent at a lower cost, helping the government reverse the cycle of ever-increasing defense budgets. Finally, Anduril made me believe that failing to develop new defense capabilities will make the United States more vulnerable to attack and less likely to win conflicts.

The Anduril founders want to leave the past behind, much as mechanized warfare left the cavalry behind in World War II. They want to drive to a new future, while navigating the ambiguity that will surely come. The founders' personal histories showed me that the team cares deeply about the mission—that their souls are in this for the long run.

Inside General Catalyst, our management committee was hesitant to invest because we were making a big and public push about responsible innovation and positive impact, yet we hadn't thought critically about how to be responsible investors in defense. But, for me, the key about the future that Anduril is building is that it can help prevent wars from starting, keep humans away from harm during battles, and defend our country at a lower cost. That makes Anduril a responsible innovation company that

The Transformation Principles

is creating a future that will benefit the world. And if the company does that well, it will generate compounding returns for its investors for a long time to come.

Creating the future is certainly harder than just improving the past. The future isn't always obvious. It doesn't come with a ready-made TAM (total addressable market) to put on a slide. Analysts don't have a quadrant to put it in. As Brian from Anduril says, "If at the start people don't think you're crazy, something's wrong. The idea is probably not revolutionary enough."

But that doesn't mean improving the past is *safer* than creating the future. This is what I learned from the mobile software company I founded. If you only improve on the past, the future will eventually arrive, and you'll be the company (or have invested in a company) that is left in the past to shrivel.

The best investments are in enduring companies that deliver returns plus positive impact. Creating a new future is key to that equation. If a company creates a new future, it has a greater chance of enduring into the future. If it creates a future that has a positive impact, it will most likely make money and increase in valuation—and do so for a long time. By that logic, investing in or founding a company that only improves the past is short-term thinking. You're leaving the future—and, thus, the greatest possible returns—on the table.

The idea that *creating a future is not a risk but a necessity* helps explain the ClassDojo story, and why I encouraged the company to take what to many outsiders looks like a precarious leap into the unknown.

Creating the Future Beats Improving the Past

When Sam Chaudhary and Liam Don founded ClassDojo in 2011, they wanted to create a new future for education—a future they could see at a time when social networks were booming and, four years after the introduction of the iPhone, smartphones were finding their way into most adults' pockets and purses.

Ever since the late 1800s, classrooms were set up to operate like factory workdays. Students arrived at the same time, did their work inside the classroom's four walls according to a schedule, then left when the bell rang at the end of the day. Parents usually didn't know what went on inside the classroom walls until a report card went home once a quarter, and teachers might never know what went on when their students weren't in the building. Life outside and inside the classroom stayed separate.

Sam and Liam believed they could use technology to stitch together a student's worlds at school and at home, knocking down the classroom's walls and creating a connected community of kids, families, and the teacher. The founders each came at this with a beginner's mind and devoted soul.

Sam grew up in a small seaside village in Wales, and while he was still in grade school, his family moved to Abu Dhabi. The international school he attended there often asked the better students—like Sam—to help teach the others. Sam went back to the UK to attend Cambridge University to become an economist, planning to get his PhD. A professor there had a friend who ran one of the oldest schools in England, which was having trouble with its economics program, and asked Sam if he'd go there and help. "The kids were amazing and the school gave me a reason to change things up," Sam says.[16] He ditched the PhD and instead went to work for an education group at consulting giant McKinsey.

The Transformation Principles

Liam was born in Germany, grew up in London, had a computer science degree and had become a game developer. He and Sam met at a hackers' contest at Cambridge, got to talking about their backgrounds—Liam's mother was a primary school teacher—and decided to work together on technology that could help kids make the most of their education. They got a spot at a tech startup incubator called ImagineK12, which became part of Y Combinator. "What came out was our mission: to give every kid an education that they love," Sam says. "So we had two problems to solve: First, how do you reach every kid on Earth? Second, how do you give each of them learning experiences they love?"

Where to start? Well, they realized that the "ed-tech" industry had focused on just selling software to schools and districts, with limited success and scale. Doing more of that didn't seem to be a promising path. But Sam and Liam had been watching powerful tech trends at the time—social networking, games, and mobile—and realized there was a big opportunity to serve consumers: the people, rather than the system. In other words: to build a consumer company, rather than yet another enterprise one.

After interviewing hundreds of teachers, kids, and families, they found that communication between these three groups was poor. So they built a classroom communications app: a way for teachers, kids, and families to connect, sharing photos, videos, moments, and messages from the school day, and creating a digital community around the classroom. They called their app ClassDojo.

I believed in them and the future they wanted to create, and I invested in the company. By mid-2016, ClassDojo was being used in two-thirds of US schools and had spread to 180 countries. By 2023, the app had an audience of 45 million kids worldwide,

Creating the Future Beats Improving the Past

making it one of the largest communities on the planet for this demographic. ClassDojo was breaking down classroom walls and reinventing school, all while operating a profitable business. The first part of the mission Sam and Liam had articulated in 2011 was coming true. And that's when they began to reach for a bolder second stage of their mission.

As Sam said to me, building a large-scale community wasn't just an ambition—it was fundamental to ClassDojo's mission. That community becomes a way to deliver services that fill gaps that schools can struggle to meet.

So, during the COVID-19 pandemic of 2020 and 2021, schools shut down and classrooms went virtual. Teachers struggled to adapt. A lot of students weren't getting the kind of attention they needed in virtual school and were falling behind. For many parents, hiring private tutors was prohibitively expensive. ClassDojo recognized that it had a massive network of students, teachers, and families and saw an opportunity to virtually match families with top tutors for a fraction of the usual cost. The service, Dojo Tutor, started as a human-to-human service and is now evolving into a human-AI hybrid tutoring model.

When school and tutoring go virtual, families face a concern about screen time, especially whether their kids are being exploited or manipulated while online. That led Sam and Liam to the belief that they could build a place online for kids that would be in the kids' best interests and not an addictive content machine—a place where they could learn, grow, and play safely with friends. No strangers, no dark corners, no cheap engagement tricks. That would turn a worry into a positive, because, in coming decades, work and life are going to move fluidly between real and virtual spaces. Safely learning how to do that as children is an advantage. As I write this, ClassDojo is testing a beta version of its virtual world—a closed space that is an extension of the classroom but also an extension of the playground, a place for kids to play, learn, and hang out together after school.

The era of the factory model of schooling is ending. In its place, a twenty-first-century hybrid model of learning is taking shape—one where the boundaries between class, life, and play blur.

To some company leaders or investors, ClassDojo's ambition could seem reckless. The company already has a product—its app—that the market wants and is adopting, with lots of room to grow. Why spend precious time and resources trying to create an unproven future? Isn't that risky? But, as I said earlier, I believe that striving to create a new future is less risky than improving the past—or, for that matter, improving the present. The company's soul is pointed at a big problem: how to bring education into the modern world. It has a future it wants to create but has the sense to know it can't predict exactly what that future will look like. It's obvious that kids will—and must—learn and socialize virtually. ClassDojo has all the pieces in place to discover that future ahead of competitors. "Our mentality is, if we think there's a better future, we should go and build it, and we should move fast," Sam says.

I'd like to hear that from every company founder.

At General Catalyst, we strive to practice what we preach, which means applying these nine principles to our company. As I've detailed already in this book, my partners and I became convinced that the venture capital industry and profit-only capitalism need to be reinvented. VC needs a new future. That means that tinkering with the traditional VC model isn't enough. We don't want to just make VC more efficient or a little bit more successful. We see an opportunity for transformation.

That's why we're taking a leap into the unknown by pairing traditional VC—a proven engine of innovation—with long-term investments and partnerships that can act as an engine of transformation.

This is manifesting first in our health assurance initiative.

To tee up a vision of the future, we at General Catalyst published the book *UnHealthcare*, which describes the future we want to create. In the book, we said we believe that there would be a need for 10 to 15 major new platforms in order to really change healthcare into health assurance—each of them a $100 billion company (as opposed to betting on finding a single trillion-dollar Amazon of health tech). To spur such massive company building, our venture capital business is investing in startups that bring healthcare innovations to life. But the opportunity exists on a much longer horizon and in more complex ways than fits into a VC structure. So we set up new capital solutions and businesses, such as creating a partnership with more than two dozen hospital systems and outright buying an Ohio hospital system, Summa Health, so tech companies have a way to deeply collaborate with incumbents, together finding ways to create a new future for healthcare that we call "health assurance." These businesses sit alongside the venture business.

While we invest in and build companies that can create a new future for our health, that process is leading us to try to create a new future that goes beyond venture capital. We are taking

The Transformation Principles

the model of innovation plus transformation that we're using for health assurance and applying it to climate tech and defense tech, and later we'll do the same with other sectors.

We are hopeful that our model will work, and if it does, others will join the movement to reinvent venture capital and capitalism itself. As the movement gains momentum, we will together create a new future and leave the old models behind.

CHAPTER FOUR

THOSE WHO PLAY THEIR OWN GAME WIN

If a company is competing, it's already losing.

Whether you're running an investment entity or a company, or pursuing a career as an individual, competing means you're constantly trying to prove that you're *better*—faster, bigger, cheaper, stronger—than those you're competing against. You have to win that argument every day. And you risk someone else coming along who claims to be even faster, bigger, cheaper, or stronger. You say your dial goes to 11; they come out with a dial that goes to 12. It becomes an arms race, or, worse, a price-cutting race to the bottom.

The more advantageous position for the long run is to be different—to play your own game, not someone else's. If you play your own game, you also get to set the rules. And if you do that, the rules will always give you an advantage if and when others try to play the same game.

The importance of playing your own game first dawned on me when I was at MIT. As described previously, I realized that most of my classmates—all supersmart top students—arrived at MIT wanting to be outliers, but instead they settled into

The Transformation Principles

familiar undergraduate patterns, working hard to get straight As in prescribed majors. I wanted to create my own journey and take courses across multiple disciplines. Some might have seen that as a bad strategy—after four years, my coursework might not add up to a degree in any single major. But it made me a different, cross-discipline thinker, which to this day helps me see connections others might miss. I played my own game and left MIT with a reputation as an outlier.

It took me a while in professional life to apply this principle to my work. I started a company based on pattern matching about mobile software. That didn't turn out well. In my rookie years as a VC, I also fell into pattern matching, making investments into discernible trends. But soon I realized that if I wanted outsized returns, I had to be anti-pattern and invest in outliers. And if I wanted outlier founders to seek me out, I, too, had to play my own game and build a reputation as a different kind of investor.

At General Catalyst, Andy Golden (as of this writing, recently retired after decades of running the Princeton University endowment) had been a limited partner and our lead investor for more than 20 years, and he's now a special advisor to GC. He has been a close friend and mentor to me. When I first made the move to Silicon Valley, I would take him down to the bar after our annual meetings and ask him, "How do I beat the Valley's legendary firms?" And he would always say to me, "Play your own game. Run your own race." I learned a lot from legendary VCs like Marc Andreessen and Vinod Khosla who had such a deep understanding and history of technology. But I knew we ultimately had to do our own thing, and I always encourage our team just not to worry about what other people are doing. If we're different, we're not competing with them. We're more like an alternative to them.

Those Who Play Their Own Game Win

That, then, becomes a different kind of choice for founders. And smart founders want to bring together investors from a number of firms and make use of our diverse perspectives.

We want to back founders who similarly play their own game. A lot of investors are in the pattern-matching business. They strive to discern hot trends in technology and find companies that fit a profile that's likely to succeed in an emerging space. It's a safe strategy for getting decent returns in a short time span. But to make outsized, compounding returns and have an impact over long time spans, investors need to find and back outliers—companies that don't fit any pattern. Sometimes these are the companies that legendarily got turned down by VCs over and over before getting funded. In 2008, a long string of investors turned down Airbnb when it was trying to raise just $150,000. (Imagine their regret now!) Some megasuccesses had even more frustrating early fundraising experiences.

Investors who back outliers don't rely on pattern matching. Instead, they rely on some version of the principles in this book. They listen to founders with a beginner's mind and assess the founders' soul along with the founders' ability to navigate ambiguity and create a new future.

As CEO of General Catalyst, I want my company to be in the anti-pattern business. Which means we have to be able to know if a founder or company is a category creator rather than a category follower.

Sometimes it's obvious. When a company references another company, saying, for instance, that it's building the "Uber for (fill in the blank)," it's a good bet the company is pattern matching, and that a dozen other companies have seen the same pattern and are working on the same thing. It's also obvious when a company's

The Transformation Principles

pitch leans on "better," as in saying that the company does what another company does, but X% faster or cheaper.

Other times, it's not immediately obvious, and we have to do some due diligence. We review thousands of pitches a year at our company, so we often have enough institutional knowledge to determine right away if a business idea is new and different. Still, we'll check it out and see if anyone is doing something similar. In the world's vast startup ecosystem, it's rare to find any idea that no one has ever thought of. But we look at so much more than just the business idea. We want to fund companies that have a good chance of creating a new market category and winning it over time. Such companies tend to have a unique point of view on how the category should work and what the product should do. And the founders must bring their soul to the mission, because soul will give them the courage to stick to their own game and believe in it when the going gets rough. And it will help them make the right decisions as they navigate ambiguity toward the future they want to create. Companies that play their own game don't end up getting distracted by what competitors are doing or by worries about short-term revenue. They make long-term decisions. The transformation principles add up and reinforce each other. Companies that live up to the principles have a good chance of enduring and generating compounding returns as they drive powerful positive change.

Great changes in technology and context open up opportunities to create new categories of products and services. The mid-2020s ushered in enormous technological change—an explosion

Those Who Play Their Own Game Win

of progress in AI, genomics, blockchain, and more—on top of social, economic, and geopolitical change.

In previous chapters, I told the stories of a couple of companies that identified a new problem that was created by a change in context and set out to solve it, initiating a new market category in the process.

One of those companies is Anduril. Its founders recognized that technology is making war and defense more about software and data than hardware, and that the incumbent defense companies are not set up to produce those kinds of solutions. The founding team intentionally set out to create a new category of defense company, hoping to influence others to join the movement. The company sees the creation of this category as a patriotic duty.

Applied Intuition also identified a new problem in a change of context. Similar to Anduril, Applied Intuition's founders understood that cars and trucks are entering a new era of being software defined, while the established automakers have always focused on hardware. Applied Intuition set out to solve this problem for the auto industry by creating a new category of software tools that automakers can use to build new-generation cars and trucks.

Advances in technology and changes in context can also open up opportunities to solve old problems in a new way—another path for a company to play its own game.

For instance, Grammarly is defining a new category by harnessing AI to solve an age-old problem: Many people struggle to communicate well in writing. Brad Hoover is now on Grammarly's board and was CEO for over a decade. He used to be an investor at General Catalyst. Grammarly was founded in 2009 in Ukraine by Dmytro Lider, Alex Shevchenko, and Max Lytvyn. The three founders first started one company to build software that could

The Transformation Principles

detect plagiarism. That company got acquired by an education tech company, Blackboard. When the founders left their first company, they started thinking: *Why do people plagiarize in the first place?* Often it's because they can't write well, or they find writing hard or tedious. Plagiarism was a symptom of a much bigger problem—people needed help with their written communication. And, since the founders are Ukrainians frequently doing business with people who speak English, they focused on writing for people who speak English as a second language. They realized they could apply AI—even though AI in 2009 was nowhere near as powerful as it is today—to solve the problem. Sure, in 2009 you could buy software that would check grammar, spelling, and punctuation, and Grammarly's product would do that. But AI made it possible for the software to understand what you were writing and do things like suggest better words or ways to be clearer. Grammarly's software can even analyze the way a piece of writing will be received by the recipient and help the writer tailor the message so it will land more effectively. Advances in AI opened up a new way to solve a problem that has existed for centuries—a solution someone could previously only get by hiring a human editor.[17]

Not long after Grammarly's launch, Brad was looking for a person to double-check his own writing, like emails. He found Grammarly's software and was blown away by the quality. Brad met the founders after using the product and partnered with them as CEO a short time later. "The initial product was targeted to students and language learners, but it was just as relevant to professionals and native English writers like me. They built an incredible product, addressing a massive need, with a strong core team. This provided a strong foundation to scale and deliver on

Those Who Play Their Own Game Win

our mission of improving lives by improving communication," Brad told me. This company was playing its own game, believed passionately in the future it wanted to create, and had a supersized global market it could win. "Communication is essential to our relationships, academic achievements, and professional endeavors," Brad says. "By helping people improve their communication, Grammarly has a huge impact on their lives."

Despite Brad's General Catalyst connection, when Grammarly needed funding, it didn't just come to us. When Brad first joined Grammarly, I didn't yet understand the scope of what they were working on. Brad came to us in 2015 and walked me through how big the business could become, and I was blown away. I was convinced Grammarly was playing its own game and was creating a new future. General Catalyst invested.

Grammarly has been a great success story. By early 2023, it had about 30 million daily users. But there are a couple of notes about Grammarly that I want to add. In February 2022, Russia invaded Ukraine, and the war, as of this writing, continues. At the time of the invasion, Grammarly's employees were spread around the world. Those in Ukraine kept working, sometimes in bomb shelters. The company donated millions of dollars to help the people of Ukraine. It's been a difficult time for Grammarly, yet the team has endured and the company has thrived—an amazing feat.

The other development about Grammarly was the late-2022 arrival of ChatGPT and the explosion in generative AI. I give Grammarly credit for quickly building generative AI into its product, which it called GrammarlyGO. The new product can learn from your writing and generate text that mimics your style.

The Transformation Principles

Grammarly, in other words, adroitly navigated ambiguity on its quest to create a new future of written communication.*

Playing your own game doesn't only mean developing new technology or building a breakthrough product. It can also be the result of building a distinguishing company culture or business model in an existing category. Merck played its own game in pharmaceuticals by putting science and research first. Ben & Jerry's played its own unique game in the premium ice cream category by creating a quirky, hippie-ish image built around its founders. I backed one company, Gusto, that has played its own game—and won—by operating with a responsible business model in the category of human resources platforms for small companies. Sticking to its own game turned out to be the key to Gusto's long-term success.

The story goes like this: Around 2014, cloud-based human resources platforms were catching on, and Zenefits was seen as the red-hot leader in hyperscale mode. From 2014 to 2015, Zenefits grew from $1 million in annual recurring revenue to $20 million, and it set a goal of hitting $100 million in 2016. Zenefits was growing so fast because it made its software free to businesses, and then it made money on commissions from health insurers and other providers on benefits sold to its customers. So, to make money and keep up the pace of growth, Zenefits' employees were under intense pressure to push products on its customers—often products the customers might not want or need. That started to

---

* In December 2024, Grammarly bought Coda and made Coda's CEO, Shishir Mehrotra, CEO of the combined company.

Those Who Play Their Own Game Win

backfire in 2016. The company ran into trouble with regulators and customers, and as the business stumbled, the company laid off half of its employees as its valuation got cut in half. Its founder and CEO, Parker Conrad, resigned.* Zenefits may have been playing its own game, but it was a treacherous game constructed on an unsustainable business model.

On the surface, Gusto, founded in 2012, was not offering a radically differentiated product from Zenefits or other newcomers to the space. But its founder, Joshua Reeves, developed a business model and culture that steered Gusto to act in a more responsible way. Gusto sells its service as a subscription. Gusto's customers have to feel they are getting good value from the service, or they will cancel. So Gusto's employees are motivated to give great customer service and build products that truly help users, not take advantage of them. Gusto developed metrics to track whether it is solving customers' problems or creating more. The company also does regular employee surveys and keeps tabs on churn and morale. If workers were to feel burned out or wouldn't recommend working at Gusto, that might indicate growth is getting ahead of the leadership team's ability to manage the company well and to keep customers happy.

However, there was a moment in 2015 when Josh pointed to Zenefits' rocketing numbers and wondered if Gusto should switch to the Zenefits "freemium" model. It looked tempting. But, again, companies that play their own game need to have the soul to stand

---

* Not long after resigning from Zenefits in 2016, Parker Conrad cofounded Rippling with Prasanna Sankar, who had been the Zenefits CTO, this time basing the company on a more responsible set of values. In 2024, Rippling was worth more than $13 billion.

The Transformation Principles

by that game in the face of short-term pressures. After some debate, Josh concluded that Gusto should believe in its long-term strategy. Not long after, that paid off. By playing its own responsible game, Gusto differentiated itself from Zenefits and others in the HR tech space, developed a reputation for caring for customers, and steadily won business. By 2023, more than 300,000 small companies were paying for Gusto software that manages payroll, health insurance, tax filing, and other HR functions. The company grew from about 1,000 employees in 2020 to nearly 2,500 in 2023. It got there by being different—not just better.

In general, the companies that play their own game are the ones that change something about the way we work and live, and they become the standouts we can name and the companies talented people aspire to work for. After decades of all sorts of smartphone designs, Apple played its own game and came out with an unproven concept: a phone with no keyboard connected to an app store. The iPhone was born and has since dominated the market. Other companies tried to make electric cars but sold them as environmentally good cars that, however, performed poorly compared to gas-powered cars. No one but hardcore environmentalists bought them. Tesla played its own game and developed an electric car that performed better than gas cars, selling it as a luxury model, and reinvented the car market. In an era when corporations bought, installed, and maintained expensive and complex software for customer relationship management (CRM), Salesforce played its own game and sold a cloud-based version of CRM that could be bought by subscription. Salesforce not only changed how companies manage sales but opened up the era of cloud computing for big business.

All of those companies took chances on a different and daring innovation, and they ended up creating more value than all the copycats put together.

The first principles in this book are informed by my life experiences, but I also live and work by them. As I said earlier, I want General Catalyst to play its own game. I'm not looking to build a *better* VC firm, I'm working to transcend venture capital, play our own game, and create something *different*.

VC tends to work on relatively short time spans—10 years at most. That's too short if we're going to use capitalism to drive powerful, positive, enduring change. And too many VC firms prioritize returns and pay less attention to whether they are funding technology or businesses that lead to harmful unintended consequences—like the way social media fuels divisiveness and conspiracy theories online. We believe that is a risky business practice—the cost of such consequences are too high.

Capitalism needs a new set of principles for our era. Investors need a new way of thinking about investing and company building.

To that end, we're developing a new category of investing and company building. This new kind of entity is structured so it can finance innovation and then scale and responsibly manage beneficial transformation through every stage over decades. It combines a system of innovation with a system of transformation under one umbrella, able to deploy committed capital in whatever way necessary to drive positive change. The goal is to shift from exit and short-term gains to endurance and long-term compounding returns.

The Transformation Principles

This new kind of entity—more of an integrated company than a traditional partnership firm—relies on venture capital as its engine of innovation. VC is matchless at launching tech companies and creating value. We don't want to lose that. The venture component will both fund amazing entrepreneurs and found companies, actively engaging in creating new innovation when it is needed to drive change. But then, the VC unit of an enduring capital company can hand off a company to a system of transformation that has time horizons far longer than ten years. This system of transformation can make acquisitions, run companies, partner with incumbents, and consult on policy—whatever it takes to deliver powerful positive change. The entire entity operates like a flywheel—scaling innovation and driving transformation through industries and society, which in turn creates demand for more innovation and ultimately generates returns that can be reinvested in greater change. It is the comprehensive, multithreaded, patient-capital approach to investing and company building that this era needs.

The long timelines encourage responsible innovation because technologies that are managed poorly and eventually create unintended harmful consequences can devastate returns and throw a wrench into the flywheel.

So, at General Catalyst, we are playing our own game by building an enduring capital company. This effort comes from my soul. Everything in my life has led up to this.

And, as I've said, we're applying this new model to the transformation of healthcare into health assurance. We have a history of success in venture capital, and that will always be our system of innovation—our core engine. So we invest in category-defining health-tech startups. We also start companies when we see an unfilled need. We acquire companies that will help us accelerate change. We partner with industry incumbents that want to be part of positive enduring change.

To truly change healthcare, we had to go beyond just investing in point solutions. The fact is that GC is one of the largest, if not the largest investor in healthcare startups in the country. Have we really improved healthcare? Go talk to anyone on the street and you'll find few believe that. We had to go deeper and build platforms for change. We've had to create a flourishing ecosystem to enable change. That starts with the health providers. They have to be willing and eager to accept change to deliver true transformation. We need the buy-in and expertise from frontline staff, and so we need them to experience how new technologies help them do their jobs better and keep patients healthier. We created convening moments to bring together technologists and health system CEOs. It takes a lot to help a very risk-averse industry sector reimagine how they can deliver care while respecting healthcare professionals' dedication to the safety and well-being of patients.

A through line in all of this is that we are working to make healthcare better, more affordable, and more accessible to far more people—because we want to make sure that change means inclusive change.

Like the founders we admire and want in our camp, we're creating the change we want to see in the world.

CHAPTER FIVE

SERENDIPITY MUST BECOME INTENTIONAL

Many companies start with a happy accident. Someone sets out to solve a problem that matters to them. They create a business or technical solution that resonates with others. The solution turns into a one-product company . . . and then, too often, a good first act doesn't evolve into a second act. The company stalls, gets acquired, or folds. An investment in such a company may result in an okay short-term return, if lucky. This is not the kind of investment I want to make or a company I'd want to build.

Most *great* companies also start with a happy accident. Then the team becomes intentional about what they're building. They turn the serendipity of an opening act into a robust second act. The second act becomes a third and a fourth—like American Express evolving from freight forwarding to travel services to financial services. The company's soul lives on through generations. The problem to solve becomes more complex and important. The initial product turns into a suite of products sold through multiple channels. Such companies evolve into an enduring presence

The Transformation Principles

in people's lives. They drive change. An investment generates returns for decades. Those are the companies I want to invest in and build.

As an investor, I can meet with an early-stage founding team and get a pretty good idea whether they live up to the first four principles in this book. Their backstory can help me understand whether they have the soul to persevere and work on solving a significant problem over the long haul. Their vision helps me believe they can navigate their way to a new future they want to create. The uniqueness of their idea and approach show me they are playing their own game.

But even when all of those traits are there and build on each other, I still need to believe that a founder will make the transition from serendipity to intentionality.

Some have that capability from the beginning. In a first meeting with a founder or founding team, I'm looking for certain signals: if they're driven by a mission they feel in their soul, if they think long-term, if they play their own game, if they see over the horizon and believe in it. I must be able to see that they are learning organisms—that they have a beginner's mind and are open to information and new ideas. Do they want to surround themselves with the best people—or with their own friends?

I knew from my first dinner with Gusto founder Josh Reeves that he had it. He told me about the first product he was setting out to build, but he also described his mission to empower small businesses and level the relationship between employer and employee—a problem that could only be solved by a company that builds a rich, multifaceted solution. He walked in with a plan, and he made me believe he would execute it for as long as it might take. Every new initiative—every product, every hire, every sale,

Serendipity Must Become Intentional

and every marketing campaign—needs to reinforce, extend, and magnify the position the company started with.

Intentionality requires discipline and design. Too often, startups chase shiny objects, building products that veer in different directions, confusing the market and sapping energy from the company.

General Catalyst was an investor in online eyeglass company Warby Parker. It started in 2010 with a happy accident. When Warby cofounder Neil Blumenthal was in college, he took a fellowship with a nonprofit, VisionSpring, that trains people to travel through developing countries checking people's eyesight. If someone needs glasses, VisionSpring can provide them for less than four dollars. So Blumenthal saw firsthand that it's possible to source prescription eyeglasses that can be sold cheaply. After college, Blumenthal enrolled in the MBA program at The Wharton School, where he met David Gilboa. Not long after they got acquainted, Gilboa left a $700 pair of Prada glasses in an airplane seat back pocket. Frustrated, Gilboa told that story to Blumenthal, and they got to talking about how they could source and sell hip, designer-style glasses online for a fraction of the cost of Gilboa's lost Pradas. The outcome of their conversation: Blumenthal, Gilboa, and two other classmates launched the Warby Parker online store.

That was the first act. The serendipity of Blumenthal's work with VisionSpring met Gilboa's problem of lost expensive glasses while they were at a business school learning how to run a company. They played their own game, creating a new category of e-commerce. But that's where it could have ended—as an online store that some consumers would see as an alternative to buying glasses through optometrists and kiosks in shopping malls.

The Transformation Principles

Warby, though, got intentional around a mission to reinvent the eyeglass industry. By selling online, Warby compiled data about who was buying and what they wanted, enabling it to sell a streamlined, curated product line—the hippest glasses at the lowest cost. Warby started out only online and would let customers try on glasses by sending them five pairs, without lenses, in the mail (which the customers would then send back). To make its glasses more accessible, its next step was to open stores so people could walk in and try on as many glasses as they'd like. As of this writing, Warby has more than 200 stores, with plans to open hundreds more. The stores then started to offer eye exams, cutting out the need for a trip to an optometrist. The Warby leadership team also invested in the nuts and bolts of the business, such as customer service. Like many companies, Warby responds to tweets about problems or questions, but Warby also started the practice of responding to a complex question by creating a YouTube video and tweeting the link, which often thrills customers so much that they then retweet it, ramping up the company's reputation on social media. Then Warby invested in manufacturing. At the beginning, it bought from third-party suppliers, but now it makes most of its own glasses, giving the company more control over quality and margins. In its next phase of reinventing the eyeglass experience, Warby is investing in telemedicine. It has already rolled out an online vision exam that lets customers get a prescription in under 10 minutes from home. The goal, as stated by Blumenthal and Gilboa, is to become a "holistic vision care company." It serves over two million customers and employs 3,000, and it went public in 2021.

Through it all, Warby has also been devoted to having a positive social impact. Of course, it is making stylish glasses available

Serendipity Must Become Intentional

to a broader population. But it also gives glasses to a person in need for every pair it sells. In New York, where Warby is based, the company worked with the mayor to create a program to send optometrists to schools and supply free glasses to students who can't afford them. Warby is expanding the program to other major cities.

Warby started out as a straightforward e-commerce company and would have stayed that way if it had not moved from serendipity to intentionality.

Serendipity to intentionality is the most common long-term success story in business. It is certainly true in technology. Bill Gates and Paul Allen were friends in Seattle who, while still high school students, got into computer programming languages. After seeing a magazine story in 1975 about the Altair 8800—one of the first personal computers on the market—they started Micro-Soft (its original name) to develop a BASIC interpreter for that machine. Their background met a budding need, and the company started with serendipity. Gates, the primary strategic driver, then became intentional. He won the right to develop the operating system for the IBM PC, introduced in 1981, and kept building on that franchise. Next came Windows in 1985. Then productivity software like Word and Excel. By then named Microsoft, the company was on a change-the-world mission that Gates stated as "a computer on every desk and in every home." The company went public in 1986. If you had invested $1,000 then, it would've been worth more than three million dollars by 2024. If Gates had not moved on from Micro-Soft's first act, the company would have had a fate

The Transformation Principles

more like VisiCalc, the company that created the first spreadsheet for PCs. Visicalc was an important software product that helped PCs catch on, but the company never had a real second act, and by 1985, it was insolvent.

Amazon started as an online bookstore because in 1994 Jeff Bezos thought books would be the easiest thing to sell to consumers on the nascent internet. Google started as just a new kind of search engine based on a research paper Sergey Brin and Larry Page wrote in college at Stanford. Brian Chesky and Joe Gebbia started "AirBedandBreakfast.com" after stumbling on the idea of renting out space on air mattresses in their apartment during popular conferences in San Francisco. (The breakfast offered was cereal, like Cap'n Crunch.) The Collison brothers started Stripe because they just wanted an easy way to accept payments on the internet. All of those businesses might have ridden out their first acts for a number of years before selling out or fading away. Instead, their leadership teams became intentional about building enduring, multifaceted companies that would reinvent the way we do things.

Because I believe in this principle, I'll get involved and try to influence portfolio companies that veer away from it. Sam Chaudhary at ClassDojo got pressure from some investors to stick with the company's first act (the classroom app) because it was getting great traction. We at General Catalyst stepped up and boosted the company's funding to help it pursue its second act (a virtual education world), which has the potential to make ClassDojo into the most significant new brand for kids since Disney. Zach Reitano at Ro was successful enough at his first act that he got offers to take the company public through a SPAC (special-purpose acquisition company) at a five-billion-dollar valuation. But I knew

Serendipity Must Become Intentional

that his intention was to transform Ro into a company that would change the healthcare experience—a much bigger goal with a much bigger potential outcome. I encouraged him not to worry about exits and stay the course. So far, it looks like the right move.

The goal for General Catalyst is to invest and build companies that drive enduring, positive change and generate compounding returns for decades. That doesn't happen with just the serendipity of a first act. It needs the intentionality of many next acts.

While most companies begin with the serendipity of a happy accident, it's also possible to begin with a dash of serendipity and a boatload of intentionality. That's the story of a company I helped launch in 2023, Hippocratic AI. Its intention is to use generative AI to eventually give every person their own personalized virtual healthcare agent and health advisor.

The story starts with a walk I took with Munjal Shah at the beginning of 2023. Generative AI was bursting onto the scene, and the two of us got to talking about how it could transform healthcare. Munjal and I had known each other for about a decade through MIT circles. Earlier in his career, he had built two AI companies, so he knew the technology. A day after he sold his second company to Google, he went running and started having chest pains. "It should have been the best day of my entrepreneurial career," he says now. "I'd sold a company for hundreds of millions of dollars. And all of the sudden I was in the emergency room." His experience as a heart patient within the healthcare system was much like it is for many Americans: maddening and expensive. (And he had the wherewithal to get the best healthcare. The

The Transformation Principles

experience for most people is far worse.) The incident drove Munjal to get serious about his health, lose more than 30 pounds, and decide he wanted to use his abilities to change healthcare. "When generative AI showed up," he says, "I thought: I'm uniquely suited to do this—to apply it to healthcare. I have all the right skills and connections. This was the opportunity."[18]

His story and determination convinced me he had the soul to follow through on his vision. On our walk, we discussed the new future he wanted to create. We landed on an urgent problem to solve. The United States alone is short about 200,000 nurses. Around 133 million Americans—nearly half the population—have some kind of chronic health condition. All of those people would have a better chance of managing their conditions if they had a personal health guide assigned to them to check on them and help them. In an ideal world, that guide would be a human nurse. No AI will ever be better than that. But the gap between the actual number of nurses and the ideal number of nurses is astronomical, with no way to close it by traditional means. It's physically not possible (there aren't enough people to become all the nurses we should have), and it's economically not possible. (How would society pay for a hundred million nurses at $90 per hour?)

Generative AI can change this situation. The solution isn't to make AI that replaces human nurses—it's to use AI agents to supersize the world's nursing staff. A generative AI can converse with people through chatbots or voice in a way that is knowledgeable and also feels almost human. And when a generative AI is intensely trained in a particular field, it can become much more accurate and trustworthy compared to a broad-based AI like the public version of ChatGPT. Munjal's concept is to intensely train a generative AI in healthcare to create as many always-on healthcare agents as the world would ever need. Such AI agents aren't going to take care of physical tasks like changing bandages or drawing blood or providing real human empathy and care—that's for the human nurses, and we'll still need as many of those as we can get. But an AI healthcare agent can regularly check on patients, converse with them, find out what's wrong, make recommendations, and, if necessary, hand off the patient to a human nurse or doctor. It is not allowed to diagnose or prescribe—that would not be safe. As an AI healthcare agent interacts with a patient, it can get to know that patient and so tailor the conversation and advice to that individual. The AI is endlessly patient and able to talk about any subject (it's read the whole internet!) in just about any language. The outcome will be that every person could have their own custom care manager in the cloud, available anytime for any question, providing a kind of pre-nursing layer that's never been able to exist, yet could make an enormous difference in people's lives and in the GDP of healthcare. Even if it just checks on patients after they get a new medication, ensuring that the medicine is taken properly and causes no side effects, that would, by itself, greatly reduce doctor and hospital visits. "I actually think this is the single most important thing we can do for health equity," Munjal says.

The serendipity here is Munjal's experience and health condition connecting to a new technology—generative AI—that has the potential to solve an age-old intractable problem. The future he wants to create is one where every person can be called on by their own virtual healthcare agent. Since this is all so new, he is playing his own game. As for navigating ambiguity, Munjal knows his solution will take shape over time. "I haven't even thought of all the things we might do when this brings us to a

The Transformation Principles

world of healthcare abundance that we have never seen before," he notes.

This is a company that has to start with a great deal of intentionality. For one thing, it's dealing with people's health. The product can't be pushed into the market until it's proven to be safe. No minimum viable product should be released—that would be too risky. Munjal chose the company name—Hippocratic AI—to reflect medicine's Hippocratic oath.

"Our AI needs its own language model, and to do it properly, it will take time to build," Munjal says. "We raised an amount of money to allow us time to make our model the definitive standard." The company teamed up with forty healthcare systems to help build the language model.

Munjal is having to think through second and third acts from the beginning. And I have no doubt that once the product is in the market, he'll quickly need to consider yet further ways to build this business. Ultimately the goal is to make a dent in one of the world's hardest problems: health equity. Everyone in the world could get an instant upgrade to their healthcare. The opportunity is as big as it gets. It may have started with the serendipity of Munjal's health crisis meeting generative AI, but it necessarily moved quickly to deep intentionality.

As you may have gathered, I, too, have learned to move from serendipity to intentionality. In my younger years, I leaned heavily on serendipity. At MIT, I took the classes that interested me without paying a lot of attention to what they would add up to. There was too much serendipity in starting a company to try to get on board

Serendipity Must Become Intentional

with the mobile device boom and too little intentionality about what to do once we got that going—resulting in the company's demise. It was serendipity that I got the chance to join a year-old VC firm, General Catalyst, as an entrepreneur in residence, and serendipity that the partners gave me a chance to start investing with the firm. After a couple of years as a VC, I realized that if I became intentional about what I was doing, I could marshal all of that serendipity for something bigger. The courses I took, scattered across different disciplines, became a strength—I could connect dots across different fields and see opportunities that others who were more narrowly focused would miss. The experiences with my startup and early investments gave me experience in what not to do—don't start a company that has no soul; don't be a pattern-matching investor. When I moved General Catalyst to Palo Alto, I also, personally, moved to intentionality. I wanted to be intentional about transforming troubled industries and intentional about making GC into a unique, category-defining investment company—an endurance capital company.

This is what anyone should do with their career. You may have relied on serendipity to shape your knowledge and experiences, but there comes a time when you need to intentionally build on that serendipity and do something significant with it.

Munjal and Hippocratic AI are part of my journey to intentionality in healthcare. At first, I was too reliant on serendipity to try to change the healthcare experience. I cofounded and invested in healthcare data company Humedica because it seemed like a good idea and I had a chance to partner with Glen Tullman, who had previously built a previous successful health-tech company. But Humedica didn't make even a dent in the healthcare experience. However, the Humedica experience led to Glen and

The Transformation Principles

me starting Livongo, offering a new cloud-based way for people with diabetes to manage their conditions. Livongo built a category and became the defining company in its space. We sold it for $18 Billion. And still, it made only a modest dent in the healthcare experience, serving about half a million of the more than 30 million people with diabetes in the United States. Livongo was a serendipitous success. We hit on something that worked for at least a niche population. But it became obvious that if we wanted to truly change healthcare, we needed to muster a concerted, complex, intentional effort. My company's partners and I, with help from others in our network, thought through how we wanted healthcare to look in 30 years, and we named that version of healthcare "health assurance" because we believe it should be focused on keeping us healthy instead of treating us after we get sick. We believe that health assurance can radically lower the GDP of healthcare—it costs less to be healthy than to be sick. And if the cost drops, more people can afford good care, leading to greater health equity. Once we had all that, we worked backward: What do we have to do now to get that started, and after that, how should we proceed?

We had to be highly intentional about our first steps, while we also knew that there would be ambiguity to navigate our way to our future vision. So, we began by raising a health assurance fund that would focus on investing in a spectrum of companies that would help make our vision a reality. We (Hemant and Kevin, along with Stephen Klasko) started writing a book, *UnHealthcare*, to paint a vision of a future we wanted to help create. An unfortunate side of serendipity fueled my desire to change healthcare. My father was suffering from the horrible disease ALS. In January 2020, he was admitted to Stanford University's hospital. The doctors had

Serendipity Must Become Intentional

to put a feeding tube and breathing tube in him to allow him to survive, and they asked me if I wanted to "pull the plug." I looked into my father's eyes and saw he wanted to live, and in that moment I felt the emotionality that causes us to make poor decisions in healthcare. He had a miserable few months because I didn't want to live with the guilt of disappointing him in that moment. The day after he passed away, pandemic lockdowns started—just as Steve, Kevin, and I were finishing *UnHealthcare*. COVID-19 laid bare the struggles of the US healthcare system, and we saw it as an opportunity to get more intentional about reshaping it. We set up partnerships with major health systems. That led to understanding (navigating ambiguity!) that incumbents can have a hard time changing, so we concluded that we would have to model the change we want to create. It all just came together and became an intentional transformation journey for me.

Everything we're doing needs to intentionally compound, helping us proactively build toward health assurance one brick at a time. Our soul is in this—health equity is a goal I've been chasing for a decade or more, and it fits with inclusive capitalism, which I believe in because of my past experiences. We are bringing aboard other similarly devoted souls, like Munjal at Hippocratic AI and Zach at Ro—a compounding of souls, if you will. We are playing our own game—this kind of concerted approach is new territory for venture capital. We are creating a future, not content to incrementally improve the existing healthcare system. And while we have a future state to animate us, we are prepared to navigate a winding path to get there.

I can tell you another story of moving from serendipity to intentionality. At General Catalyst in the early 2020s, we knew that our culture and our future would be built on the transformation principles in this book. We knew that our goal was to reinvent industries for the twenty-first century to make them more successful, more positively impactful, and more equitable around the world. One part we didn't know yet was how we'd take our mission global.

In 2022, Jeannette zu Fürstenberg, founder of Berlin-based venture firm La Famiglia, invited me to one of her events. I already needed to be in Europe at that time, so I accepted and gave a fifteen-minute talk on my view on geopolitics, global resilience, and its effect on investing—not something Jeannette had even asked me to speak about. But it struck a chord with Jeannette. We realized—serendipity at work!—that we had the same vision and ambition around re-globalization and transformational investing. Jeannette wasn't looking to exit her firm; we were not looking to merge with anyone. But the serendipitous alignment was too close. We both couldn't ignore it.

We turned that serendipity into intention, realizing that combining forces would be our path to global positive transformation. We combined in 2023. Creating a global entity then became an intentional strategy. Since we were going global, I wanted General Catalyst to do more in India. But figuring out the right investment path took time—India is unique in so many different ways. I had known Neeraj Arora for years. In the 2010s, he was chief business officer at WhatsApp, and in 2014 he cofounded a venture capital firm in New Delhi called Venture Highway. I had started spending more time in India after the pandemic and realized the opportunity at hand, and the Venture Highway team's insight into the right model for startups for India was uniquely Indian yet had a global perspective. Informed by combining with La Famiglia and driven by our new intentionality, Neeraj and I

Serendipity Must Become Intentional

started talking about bringing Venture Highway into the GC family. The Venture Highway team joined our team in mid 2024.

While many VC firms operate globally, we realized the power of a global platform because we took a serendipitous alignment of values, vision, and ambition and turned it into an intentional strategy. Now we have teams in many of the most important markets in the world, with local leaders who know those markets and act locally while sharing the broader vision and philosophy of General Catalyst.

Three decades ago, our original founders built a successful venture capital firm. But a VC firm that's like most other VC firms isn't going to change much about our industry. The soul of ours is pointed at the problem of making capitalism better, so it is inclusive and responsible, drives positive change, and focuses on endurance, not exit. If that's our future vision, we must become highly intentional about how we're going to create that future. Codifying the principles by which we operate and publishing them in this book is part of the effort. As we expose our mission and values, people who believe in what we're doing and how we're doing it will seek us out, compounding our talent pool and adding momentum to this flywheel.

A soul, a vision, uniqueness, serendipity—these are all vital to getting started on a mission to drive change. Intentionality is how you execute over and over and compound your successes to make sure that change happens.

CHAPTER SIX

FOR GREAT CHANGE, RADICAL COLLABORATION BEATS DISRUPTION

No investor, founder, or company can alone transform an entire industry, much less society.

"Disruption" was the mindset of a previous generation of tech startups and investors. But that is a go-it-alone attitude, as if saying: "Our little band of pirates can bring down a whole sector and force it to change." Disruption brought us some great innovations, but it has also led to destruction—of jobs, towns, lives, businesses, and even civil society. Disruption stirs resentment and resistance from incumbents. It does a better job of tearing down than building up. (Technological disruption blew up traditional journalism, for example, and left a gaping hole in public discourse.)

I don't invest in disruption, per se. If a founding team comes in with a stated goal of disrupting something, I get turned off.

Disruption needs to be disrupted, so to speak, by radical collaboration. I encourage and invest in radical collaboration. My company is building systems of radical collaboration, starting with health assurance and moving into climate and defense.

In my experience, most stakeholders in existing industries

The Transformation Principles

welcome positive change that makes their businesses and lives better, yet incumbents can get pinned down by the gravity of how their industry works and its business models, regulations, shareholder expectations, and expensive investments in things like factories, software, and people. For example, everyone in healthcare knows that healthcare is dysfunctional, but they feel trapped in a complex system that no single entity can overhaul. Big oil companies are fully aware of climate change but strain to shift away from carbon. Educators know that the common classroom-based school system, designed more than a century ago, isn't keeping up with changes in society and technology, but they feel powerless to completely transform that model.

Lobbing "disruptive" innovations like random hand grenades into such large, established, and important sectors usually only changes things on the fringes. Those who work on the inside, who have spent their lives in their professions, get the sense that outsiders are invading and telling them they are outmoded or worthless, so they understandably push back. They might outright reject the innovation—or lobby to get policymakers to regulate the innovation away. Systemic transformation gets throttled when these disruptors fail to work *with* the system.

Radical collaboration, on the other hand, means engaging with all the stakeholders in an existing sector and helping them change in ways they *want* to change. It requires working hand in hand with incumbents, being empathetic about their challenges, and becoming welcomed on the inside. It means understanding the role of policy and working with regulators and lawmakers to help modernize those policies. It requires significant, patient investment of capital and time—more capital and time than a typical VC fund allows. Most of all, radical collaboration demands systems thinking—knowing that any system is made up of many, many parts that all affect each other, and that they all have to change to create powerful, positive transformation.

I came to believe in the principle of radical collaboration later in my career, once I was taught a harsh lesson by the energy sector.

Around 2006, after a few years of investing in software companies like most other VCs, I applied the principles in this book to begin to change my career path. I knew I had to play my own game, not everyone else's. I wanted to create a new future, not just improve on the past. I wanted to invest in a way that mattered to my soul. For all of this, I relied on a beginner's mind—I wanted to invest in a sector that I didn't already know well, but that mattered to me, and be free to take chances others wouldn't because they supposedly knew better. I chose to get into clean energy technology ... at a time when few VCs were interested in funding cleantech.

And, basically, I lobbed grenades. I invested in a cleantech company called Gridco Systems. As a tech investor looking at the energy sector from the outside, it seemed like a very promising company. The founder, Naimish Patel, realized that individual customers of electric utilities were putting solar panels on rooftops and sending power back into the grid—a dynamic that grids weren't designed to handle. Gridco saw an opportunity to develop internet-style switches and software for the electric grid, which would make the grid capable of two-way traffic and better able to manage fluctuations in usage. But as right as the concept might have been, Gridco ran into a utility-sector culture that is wary of innovation. Regulators and executives focus on egalitarian access to energy and on reliability. That keeps the lights on nearly 100% of the time but discourages risk while incentivizing

The Transformation Principles

safety and predictability. Gridco couldn't get on the inside to help the utilities change. By 2018, the company had raised $54 million from my company and others but couldn't sustain the business and ceased operations. As industry publication *Greentech Media* wrote at that time: "Utilities have failed so far to expand their use of distribution grid-level power electronics much beyond the pilot phase, leaving Gridco with little opportunity to grow to the scale necessary to maintain its operations on the strength of its own revenues."[19]

I helped throw a couple of other cleantech grenades at about the same time, including a solar panel company called Stion, which also couldn't get traction and was a victim of cheap panels coming from China. That one ceased operating in 2017.

However, my cleantech failures led me to see the need for radical collaboration in order to create transformational change. I was still living in the Boston area, and Deval Patrick had just been elected governor. He encouraged me and other investors and entrepreneurs to develop policy ideas around transforming energy, and he wanted us to help entrepreneurs figure out how to build businesses in the energy sector. Market certainty is a big thing when you build a business, and the way the policies were written at that time didn't create market certainty for anyone coming in with innovative concepts. So, I helped found the New England Clean Energy Council, made up of people from the energy industry, investors, academics, and policymakers. We helped develop legislation, including Massachusetts's Green Jobs Act of 2008, which provided funding and mechanisms to create clean-energy businesses and jobs.

In 2011, once I moved to Silicon Valley, I helped start a public policy organization called Advanced Energy Economy. A cofounder was Tom Steyer, the hedge fund manager and political activist. Within about six years, AEE was operating in 30 states, focusing on how to align regulations with energy business models to support innovation. Because of the lessons I learned in cleantech, I understood that a good business wasn't enough—policy, technology, and finance all had to align to create an atmosphere for adoption.

Still, our collaborations at the time turned out to be too little, too late. We got a lot of cleantech companies off the ground, but they didn't transform the energy sector, and most of the companies withered. When you start compounding technology risks and market risks, getting traction takes longer, which turns off investors. New funding dries up and the companies run out of money to keep operating.

Now I apply the principle of radical collaboration in a much more systematic way. That's manifested in the way General Catalyst has worked to transform healthcare into health assurance.

A company I funded called Homeward embodies the principle of radical collaboration in the healthcare sector.

The company's cofounder and CEO, Jennifer Schneider, grew up in Winona, Minnesota, a town of about 26,000 residents on the banks of the Mississippi River. Her father ran a business called Motor Parts & Equipment, which was started by her grandfather in 1955. The company delivered parts all over rural Minnesota—if something broke, MPE got a call, and someone drove the part out to wherever it was needed. For Jennifer, seeing that as she grew up turned out to be crucial to her thinking about healthcare in rural markets. As she told me, "If you break your arm, no one goes to you to fix it." Also important was her own health experience. When she was 12, she was diagnosed with type 1 diabetes. Because of scarce healthcare in her region, it took weeks for her to first see an endocrinologist. Later, when she went to medical school at Johns Hopkins University, Jennifer was alarmed to learn how dangerous it is for someone with her diagnosis to have to wait so long to get treatment. Since 20% of the US population lives in small rural towns like Winona, tens of millions of people are stuck living with this kind of dangerous healthcare gap.[20]

Jennifer became a physician but then realized she wanted to have a bigger impact on healthcare than a sole practitioner could achieve. She joined Livongo, the company I helped found to change the way diabetes is treated, as chief medical officer and later became president. After Livongo was sold, Jennifer started working with us at General Catalyst to figure out how to positively transform rural healthcare. Rural healthcare was getting eviscerated. "About eighty percent of rural counties lack a sufficient number of primary care providers, and nine percent of rural counties have no primary care providers at all," she says. "When someone with a minimum-wage job who is paid by the hour has to take off a day and drive one hundred miles to see a doctor—that just doesn't work. So people in rural areas don't get the care they need. They have a higher mortality rate than their counterparts in cities."

Jennifer borrowed from her father's ethos: The solution is to take healthcare to the people who need it, wherever they are. She and GC created Homeward together, along with her ex-Livongo colleague, Amar Kendale. Taking a disruptive approach, à la "move fast and break things," would never work. The problem of

Radical Collaboration Beats Disruption

rural healthcare is too big. Homeward needed the cooperation of a range of stakeholders. As Jennifer explains, when Homeward decides to start serving a particular town, the company first sends representatives there to understand what's needed, where it can deliver care, and what doctors and clinics are already in town or nearby. If, for instance, a local tractor supply store has extra space, Homeward might partner with the store and set up a clinic there. Or Homeward might set up a mobile clinic in the post office parking lot. When someone signs up for Homeward, a medical professional goes to that person's home and, when appropriate, sets up connected technology—maybe a heart monitor or a glucometer or fall-detection wrist monitor—that can send relevant data back to Homeward's medical team. The company operates using value-based care, much like Cityblock Health from earlier in this book. It takes fixed payments from Medicare (currently Homeward only serves patients with Medicare plans) to keep patients healthy. The more information Homeward has about each patient, and the easier it is for patients to see someone and get help when they have a problem, the more likely it is that patients will stay healthy, stay out of hospitals, and keep medical costs down. The more Homeward can keep costs below the fixed payment, the more money it makes, sharing the savings with the insurer—a win-win for both.

Homeward's mission is to keep people healthy, not treat serious medical issues. For those, it works with the area's medical community, referring patients to specialists, helping those patients get an appointment, and providing the specialists with data or other information that can speed diagnosis and treatment. "Deep partnerships are the only way to do it," Jennifer tells me. "We can use technology to scale and serve more people, but healthcare

The Transformation Principles

is relational. Earning trust is critical. We are embedded in the community."

Jennifer adds: "The current healthcare system in rural America is fundamentally broken, but we can't throw it out. We can, though, rearrange it. We will succeed when we've changed the healthcare model for rural America." And that is a huge opportunity. "How big a business can this be? If I screw everything up, it can still be ten billion dollars."

Now consider that Homeward is only a part of a much larger health assurance movement that we're driving with radical collaboration. My takeaway from flailing away at the energy sector was that the way to create enduring, profound change is to work with existing players and help the system change. By themselves, single companies like Homeward or Cityblock or Hippocratic AI can only change the edges of something as huge and complex as healthcare.

Even if we fund loads of healthcare tech companies that are each trying to change one aspect of healthcare—and to date, General Catalyst has funded around 150—it still won't make a dent unless the incumbent healthcare community embraces the innovations and then changes their practices and processes and economic models so the whole healthcare experience transforms. Decades of health-tech startups have introduced technology that ranges from electronic medical records to telehealth to remote monitoring, but they have left the frustrating, costly US healthcare system largely intact. If an innovation doesn't fit into the common economic model of American healthcare, where patients or insurers pay for every office visit, procedure, pill, and bandage, it will die on the vine. If insurance won't pay for it, doctors and patients won't use it.

Radical Collaboration Beats Disruption

And yet, systematically reinventing important economic sectors is the most breathtaking long-term opportunity of our era. That opportunity is a major reason I'm trying to change the nature of capital. As a company, if we're going to drive enduring, systemic transformation, we need venture capital to fund early-stage companies to get innovation off the ground, but then we need patient, long-term capital and radical collaboration to take over and integrate those innovations into the sector and build on them over time.

In healthcare, we're doing that by creating a consortium of healthcare incumbents, the Health Assurance Ecosystem. As I write this, 23 health systems in four countries have joined. We brought in Marc Harrison, the former CEO of Intermountain Healthcare, and Daryl Tol, former president of AdventHealth, to run it. Both have been leaders in the existing healthcare industry. They have credibility with insiders that a startup founder might struggle to win. The consortium will act as a bridge between traditional health systems, startups, and investors. Members will be able to connect to startups and act as proving grounds for new products and services. As mentioned earlier, we're also buying a health system in Ohio, Summa Health, and creating a new company called HATCo, which stands for Health Assurance Transformation Company. Marc and Daryl run HATCo, and it will act as our showcase for collaboration, showing the rest of the sector how we can all work together to reinvent healthcare.

By working with healthcare systems and better understanding their needs and challenges, investors and entrepreneurs will be able to see gaps in technology that suggest new companies that can be built. The consortium is big enough so that when an innovation gets traction there, it can have an influence on payers such as insurance companies, encouraging them to create ways to reimburse health systems and patients when they use new solutions. As patients encounter innovations that make their care experience better, keep them healthier, or save their lives, they will demand them, creating pull from the marketplace. And as health systems see that there is a way for them to become better, more sustainable businesses while aligning more closely with the needs of patients, they'll be incentivized to adopt new technologies and practices that lead to health assurance. We have to create a movement that is attractive yet challenging. It can't be lip service. But I'm astonished by the energy of those that do join us. We thought we would bring the innovation, and they would bring the care delivery, but often they are the ones who think differently about care, and they have ideas to pitch to us—they just needed a partner that could make these things happen.

All in all, this is radical collaboration on a big scale, with a goal of long-term, fundamental change. But it's also how individual companies and investors should think. The path to powerful positive change does not go through disruption from the outside. It comes through systematic change from the inside.

How, then, should someone think about radical collaboration when making investment decisions?

If a startup founder comes in with a story about disrupting this or that, alarm bells should go off. Talking of disruption is by now a cliché. It smacks of not being thoughtful. It also means the company is going to face opposition and backlash—from incumbents, policymakers, communities, and sometimes even from customers.

Radical Collaboration Beats Disruption

Look at the battles Uber has had to fight against taxis and cities. Or go back in time to when Napster was going to disrupt the record industry and then got sued into oblivion over copyright infringement. (Music moved online only once Apple worked with the industry to create iTunes.) Sure, a disruptive company can create value, but it's less likely to drive enduring, positive change, and so it's less likely to generate compounding returns over time. Not my kind of investment.

On the other hand, it's impressive—if rare—when a founder comes in with a plan developed around radical collaboration. Those founders also likely come with soul—with love for the sector they want to help transform—and with a desire to help create a new and better future. They are more likely to facilitate enduring change and succeed over decades. Those are my kind of investments.

Such is the story of Applied Intuition, the company making software tools that help automakers build software-driven vehicles. CEO Qasar Younis is a product of the auto industry in Detroit. He understands it in his core. Automobiles are a $2.9 trillion industry globally. Nobody is going to disrupt it. Tesla accomplished the near miracle of pushing the incumbent automakers to develop electric cars. But Tesla isn't killing off the world's major auto companies. Qasar understands that the incumbents see the change to electric and autonomous vehicles coming and want to be a part of it. Applied Intuition's approach is to understand what the automakers need in order to do that and supply them with the tools that will help get them there. "If we build a horizontal company building tools for all these companies, it gets our foot in the door with very large companies," Qasar says. "Anyone making physical vehicles is looking to make them autonomous and electric. We can ride that wave. We're enabling the entire industry."[21] That is radical collaboration, and it tells me that Applied Intuition is likely to generate compounding returns for a very long time.

Berlin-based Helsing is another company that began with radical collaboration in mind, with the ambitious goal of protecting Europe's democracies. Cofounder and CEO Torsten Reil started out as a biologist, got a master's in AI, created a hugely successful iPhone game, and had semiretired to invest in deep-tech startups. Around 2021 he found himself increasingly worried that Europe's democracies were falling behind in technology, especially software and AI as it applied to defense. Like the founders of Anduril, Torsten understood that defense was increasingly going to be driven by software, not hardware, and that incumbent European defense contractors had long histories in hardware, not software. As Torsten started exploring what could be done about this, he met with two others who had experience with software and defense: Gundbert Scherf (from 2014 to 2016, he was a special representative in the German Federal Ministry of Defence) and Niklas Köhler (previously cofounder of an AI research firm, collaborating with leading defense companies). They talked of threats, anticipating Russia's president, Vladimir Putin, would invade Ukraine. "Within about thirty minutes, we said we should start a company together," Torsten says. "There was a real sense of urgency."[22]

The core purpose of Helsing is the epitome of radical collaboration. They, as Torsten says, "use software to make existing assets much more capable than they currently are." Similar to Applied Intuition in the auto industry, Helsing's goal is to make software and AI that goes into the hardware Europe's defense companies

Radical Collaboration Beats Disruption

are already building. Instead of disrupting Europe's defense incumbents, Helsing is out to make them better. While Torsten can only say so much about what its software does, he explains that by giving a fighter jet AI, the jet can interpret threats and help its pilot make split-second decisions about which countermeasures to take.

"The existing prime defense contractors in Europe build exquisite hardware," Torsten notes. "But hardware companies—any kind of hardware company—can find it difficult to build the highest-performing software teams. So Helsing is a software-first company. We can build exquisite software and partner with the existing ecosystem." Because Helsing is taking this collaborative approach, and because we believe in its mission, General Catalyst invested.

The Helsing and Applied Intuition stories highlight another benefit of radical collaboration: Such companies gain inside knowledge of what's missing amid the context of change. A company that sits on the outside bent on disruption gets shut out by the incumbents. It has to infer what's going on inside the industry, and it may never see opportunities to build products that help that industry change. Radical collaboration gets a company invited inside, giving it deep insights into what works, what doesn't, and what's still missing.

That's also the lesson we applied at General Catalyst as we moved deeper into our collaborations with healthcare systems. We realized that waiting for founders to come to us with interesting innovations wouldn't be enough. We started seeing that there were missing pieces of technology that would be needed for the whole system to change. That, in turn, led to us recruiting founders to help us start companies to address those needs.

The Transformation Principles

One of them, as an example, was Commure. While startups were building myriad products that generate data about patients—data that, when combined, can help doctors diagnose and treat their patients—no open platform existed to interoperate with all those products and assemble all that data. We started Commure to build one and are tapping into our health system coalition to prove it out. Commure is not just a company collaborating with incumbents—it's actually a product of radical collaboration.

Radical collaboration does not only mean working with incumbent companies. It means working with all stakeholders, which includes communities, consumers, and policymakers. All have to be on board if there is to be powerful, positive, enduring change. Homeward, for instance, is working to win over the rural communities in which it operates. If you don't get a warm reception in a small town, it's tough to do business there. Some sectors, such as energy and healthcare, are deeply influenced by regulations. Innovation can't help those sectors change if long-standing regulations—put in place for different times and circumstances—get in the way. Radical collaboration means working with policymakers to help them understand and guide innovations in a beneficial way.

One company we ran across, Re:Build Manufacturing, is taking a radical collaboration approach to fixing a hard, complex, multi-stakeholder problem: how to rejuvenate American manufacturing.

One of Re:Build's cofounders, Jeff Wilke, grew up in Pittsburgh, Pennsylvania, just as that city's fabled steel industry went into decline, overtaken by overseas competition. He remembers driving along the rivers that intersect at Pittsburgh and seeing the hulking, empty steel plants. As the plants closed, families lost their incomes. Stores and restaurants closed. The whole city suffered.

Jeff moved away from Pittsburgh and wound up at Accenture and AlliedSignal and then worked at Amazon for 22 years, building out and then running its entire retail operations, which honed his ability to run operations that involve both machines and lots of people. All along, Jeff's thoughts kept going back to the plant closings in Pittsburgh and to other US communities devastated by the loss of manufacturing. As he noted, "People don't move as fast as capital." As investment and wealth moved out of traditional manufacturing communities, most of the people remained stuck in those places, with their job opportunities fading. "I was worried the country was heading for a position that would not be good if we are not making things on our shores," Jeff says.[23]

He decided to do something about it. Back in 1991, Jeff had joined a program at MIT now called the Leaders for Global Operations program.* There, he met Miles Arnone, who had built a machine toolmaker and then worked with private equity firms, buying and selling manufacturing businesses. In 2020, as the pandemic closed down the world and highlighted the vulnerability of global supply chains, Jeff and Miles founded Re:Build. The need to energize US manufacturing had become even more evident. Re:Build was designed to collaborate with US manufacturers to help them adopt new technology, develop and make new products, and build new plants across the country.

---

* I had also done this program at a different time. Funny enough, Jeff and I shared the same faculty advisor.

The Transformation Principles

The ultimate goal of Re:Build, as Jeff put it, is to "have enough capability so that any company in the US that is designing and building a technically complex physical thing can come to us for everything from design to engineering through production. That could be, for instance, new aerospace inventions, electric scooters, trucks, novel biotech products, or new kinds of power generation like fusion." As of this writing, Re:Build has acquired and assembled thirteen companies that range from high-end engineering services to software design to making high-tech components. All of them are in the United States. A manufacturer can come to Re:Build and work with one of its companies or with many of them. This way, American companies don't have to get technical help or parts from overseas.

Re:Build also believes that the United States has to develop a workforce that can build world-class manufacturers going forward. So, the company committed resources to nurturing the next generation of manufacturing talent through vocational training and apprenticeships. Today, these apprenticeship programs emphasize critical trades—electrical and pipefitting, equipment assembly, and welding.

To me, Re:Build leverages radical collaboration in multiple directions. It is buying companies and creating a system of collaboration among them. It is bringing in manufacturers as customers and working with them to make them better—very different from setting up a business to disrupt existing players. When I encountered Re:Build, Jeff and Miles were not looking for capital. But the company's belief in this principle and the way it is acting on that belief led Re:Build to invite us to be a part of it. Even though Re:Build said no to a lot of other VC investors, Jeff and Miles ended up feeling that our missions were aligned, and they said yes

Radical Collaboration Beats Disruption

to us. Today Re:Build employs 1,100 people in 12 communities around the United States and brings in several hundred million dollars a year in revenue.

As a leader of my company, I believe that a key to radical collaboration is diversity of thought and a beginner's mind that is open to ideas and concepts that others bring. We're very intentional about this at General Catalyst. It's why we—atypical of a VC firm—brought in Fortune 500 business leaders such as Ken Chenault, Ken Frazier, and Lieutenant General Scott Howell, who retired from the United States Air Force in August 2021 after a 34-year career. As we built up our health assurance initiative, we brought in hospital CEOs such as Marc Harrison and Stephen Klasko. We joined with Berlin VC firm La Famiglia to help us better understand and collaborate in Europe, and we did the same with Venture Highway in India. When we look for investors in our funds, we want those who bring not just capital but interesting thinking.

As I'm finishing this book, we're going a step further: General Catalyst formed core partnerships with McKinsey, J.P. Morgan, and Amazon. In September 2024, we launched the General Catalyst Institute, led by Teresa Carlson, who previously led the public sector division at Amazon's AWS Worldwide. GCI's top priority will be to work with and serve as a trusted partner to governments and public policy leaders on how to respond, leverage, and adopt cutting-edge technology, like applied AI, during these transformative times. GCI is leaning on GC's investors and thought leaders in industry, academia, and policy to present a road map for industry transformations that drive global resilience.

The Transformation Principles

All in all, General Catalyst is becoming a strategic conglomerate—a platform for radical collaboration. All its pieces together drive what we're doing, while our company builds a culture that activates all of this diverse thought and encourages everyone to absorb it and collaborate.

On my personal journey, I always look to surround myself with people who can teach me. I don't want my success to lead to failure because I ossify into thinking that what I've done before will always work again. The best results come from keeping an open mind, accepting ideas that align with our values and principles, and creating value that is shared with collaborators and society.

CHAPTER SEVEN

CONTEXT CONSTANTLY CHANGES, BUT HUMAN NATURE STAYS THE SAME

Every business operates in a context. Context is everything that is happening in the world around the company. It includes the technologies that are available, economic circumstances, geopolitics, social mores, weather, demographics, fashion, and everything else that defines each moment in time.

And context constantly changes. New technologies get invented and old ones get bypassed. Geopolitics get upended by a pandemic or war, rippling across supply chains, markets, and business relationships. The zeitgeist shifts with every news report, viral video, policy change, and hot new trend that will probably disappear as fast as it arrived.

Every successful business is a right fit for its context. Yes, I want a company to create a new future, but it has to be a future that builds on today's context and anticipates the next one. If it's out of sync with its context—too far ahead, too far behind, or just wrong—no matter how brilliant the innovation, it won't get traction. (Remember the Segway? Brilliantly engineered breakthrough that was completely out of step with the context of its time—or, apparently, any time.)

The Transformation Principles

But there is an interesting tension between context and human nature, because while context constantly changes, human nature remains constant. Sure, there are cultural differences across borders, social groups, and history, but the deep, core drivers of human nature are always the same. Think of the seven deadly sins: pride, lust, anger, gluttony, envy, sloth, and covetousness (i.e., desire). They were as true in the time of Shakespeare as they are in the time of Taylor Swift. Or consider Maslow's hierarchy of needs, starting with basics like food and shelter and moving up to safety, love, self-esteem, and self-actualization. No matter how much context shifts, our sins and our needs remain intact. We just go about acting on them in new and different ways.

One bit of evidence of how human nature stays the same despite enormous shifts in context comes from a Harvard University study that tracked 724 participants from all over the world from 1938 to the present. The study's chief conclusion was that throughout the decades, across cultures and distance and great societal and technological change, relationships and connection make people happier than anything else. In 2023, Robert Waldinger, who most recently headed the study, published a book about the findings, titled *The Good Life*. Here's a telling passage:

> The idea that healthy relationships are good for us has been noted by philosophers and religions for millennia. In a certain way, it is remarkable that all through history people trying to understand human life keep coming to very similar conclusions. But it makes sense. Even though our technologies and cultures continue to change—more rapidly now than ever before, fundamental aspects of the human experience endure. When Aristotle developed the idea of eudaimonia, he was

Context Constantly Changes

drawing on his observations of the world, yes, but also on his own feelings; the same feelings we experience today. When Lao Tzu said more than twenty-five centuries ago "The more you give to others, the greater your abundance" he was noting a paradox that is still with us. They were living at a different time, but their world is still our world.[24]

When I evaluate a potential investment or consider building a company, I try to keep these competing truths in mind. I try to understand the company amid a changing context—is it too far behind, too far ahead, missing the point, or right on target? And I try to think through the constant role human nature will play: Will the innovation I'm looking at help us positively climb the hierarchy of needs, or will some of the seven deadly sins take the innovation down a darker path? The concept of responsible innovation is all about proactively asking the question: "What could go wrong?"* If an innovation enables any of the seven deadly sins, something will surely go wrong. I stayed away from investing in cryptocurrencies early in their existence because their killer app was greed, and indeed greed is what has driven much of that sector—to its detriment. In another classic example of human nature, every new media technology quickly gets hijacked by lust. The porn industry is always one of the early adopters. (The industry is already beginning to create AI-generated porn stars.) Social media, such as Instagram, unleashed envy and covetousness, making teenagers who aren't gorgeous and rich feel inadequate.

---

* I wrote about this, also with Kevin Maney, in our book *Intended Consequences: How to Build Market-Leading Companies with Responsible Innovation*, published by McGraw Hill in 2022.

The Transformation Principles

Anonymous internet commenting got swamped by anger because people found they could show their true human nature without consequence.

Just because something can go wrong doesn't mean an innovation has no merit. Yet the transformation principles rest on the idea that companies that have a powerful positive impact also generate the greatest long-term returns. Understanding how an innovation might be hijacked by the worst of human nature, and creating mechanisms to avoid that, is critical for a company that wants to ensure it has a positive impact and generates compounding returns for generations.

Earlier in this book, I told the story of Grammarly, which uses AI to help people write more effectively. Grammarly is a product of its context. It couldn't have created its offering ten years ago, before AI became good enough. Yet the company started building its product well before ChatGPT burst onto the scene, which gave Grammarly a head start. The company got its technology context just right, helping it stay in sync with its time. Grammarly also gets it right about human nature. We are wired to communicate and connect (as the Harvard study showed), and the better we communicate, the more we'll achieve in life and the happier we will be. Grammarly helps people climb the hierarchy of needs. I suppose people could use Grammarly to more effectively craft harmful messages, such as scams or misinformation. But what could go wrong seems minimal and containable compared to how much it helps people.

Ro, also described earlier, is another story of getting context and human nature right. Ro came to life in 2017 because of context: It couldn't have offered erectile dysfunction medication before the patent on Viagra ran out, and society before that time

Context Constantly Changes

was not yet used to blatant marketing of ED meds, which started to change thanks to commercials for drugs like Cialis blanketing television. And Ro got human nature right: If we can have more and better sex, we'll take it!

This combination of context and human nature is exactly what led General Catalyst to invest in two defense companies—Helsing and Anduril—at a time when venture capitalists mostly avoided anything to do with defense. I told both companies' stories earlier. In order to invest in them, we first had to come to an important realization that centered on human nature: Humans always have and always will use aggression to get what they want. Not all humans, of course, but enough that it will always be a threat. War has forever been intertwined with the story of civilization, and it's not going away. So, if that's true, it becomes morally sound to invest in technology that helps deter war and to invest in technology that, in the event of war, minimizes the human cost.

The founders of both Anduril and Helsing see it that way too. "I don't like the use of force—it's an undesirable way to get your way, and it is the lowest common denominator," says Helsing CEO Torsten Reil. "I believe in liberal democracies and that we have to be prepared to defend them. If an opponent uses threats, we have to have a deterrent in our back pocket. But as a democracy, we have to deal with such capabilities in an ethical and responsible way. If these technologies need to exist, then they should be developed by people who take the responsibility very seriously."[25]

"When we think of what we're trying to do, the topic that comes up is Taiwan," says Brian Schimpf, CEO of Anduril. "Our view is the goal is not to win a war with China over Taiwan. It's not a winnable situation. So the goal is to prevent it from happening in the first place. We want to put technology in place that gives China a lot of pause, and for Taiwan, gives them the ability to respond to a larger force if necessary. The idea is to create the right signal that an invasion would be hard—the right signal that might prevent conflict."[26]

If that's the human nature side, here is where context comes into play: Until recently, the most effective way to build up a defensive force was to invest in offensive weapons—hardware such as fighter jets, tanks, battleships, and missiles. These could take years, if not decades, to design and build, and they cost millions of dollars each. A single F-35 stealth fighter jet costs about $400 million. But in the 2020s, the context has been shifting. AI has become powerful enough to be a game-changer in war. It can help coordinate assets, spot threats faster than any human could, and guide weapons such as drones so military personnel can stay safely away from the battle. At the same time, advances in electronics make it cheaper and easier to build small, smart weapons like drones and robots. Unlike an F-15 jet, these can be churned out quickly and deployed in a hot zone like Taiwan or Ukraine. And indeed the war in Ukraine has become part of the context shift, proving the great value of small, smart weapons. The Ukrainian military terrorized and confounded the invading Russian army early in the war by strategically attacking it with small, smart weapons.

Put it all together, and Anduril and Helsing—and other companies pursuing similar paths in the defense software sector—understand that defense is going through a massive context shift from hardware as the advantage to software as the advantage. Both are software-first companies, a significant contrast

Context Constantly Changes

to traditional military contractors that build hardware and then write some software to operate it. Anduril's technology can help military leaders manage a battlefield buzzing with smart weapons and is building its own AI-enabled small, smart weapons. Helsing builds AI-driven software that can go into existing weapons systems to make them as much as ten times more effective. By 2024, much of the tech ecosystem was recognizing this shift in context and internalizing the idea that some subset of humans will forever resort to armed aggression, and it's morally right to defend against that. As a result, investment has poured into software-first defense startups, and these companies are pulling in top-tier talent.

Most people focus on the short term. Profit-only capitalism encourages and even demands short-term thinking. But a short-term thinker easily misses the implications of context and human nature. Such a person only sees the current context—not where it's been or where it's going—and probably misses the fact that context always changes and is going to change for any given company. Such a person also may look at the way people are behaving now and believe that the cause of that behavior is something about the current context, missing the fact that human nature stays constant and is only enabled and amplified by new technologies and societal conditions.

As I was growing up, the culture around me in India, including my studies and my family, immersed me in long-term thinking. Hindus believe that our lives are but one stop in an endless journey—a belief that encourages thinking not only about one's

The Transformation Principles

own lifespan but beyond it. Context is only the now, and it forever changes. At the same time, I was taught from when I was a boy to know the worst of human nature in myself and learn to control it and not fall prey to temptation—to the seven deadly sins. I also understood the importance of striving for security, connection, self-awareness, and self-actualization. This shaped my personality. Now, I don't let the highs and lows of business and life get to me. I think those around me would acknowledge that I stay even-keeled, always aware of and moderating the worst that human nature can bring out in me or in others. I have come to believe that the most important personal trait in business is the ability to form and maintain productive relationships, and General Catalyst's most important competitive advantage is, in fact, its relationships.

And yet, I don't think I fully comprehended the importance of context and human nature in business until, as a potential investor, I encountered the founders of Snapchat, now called Snap.

Lots of social media companies already existed by the 2010s. But during a meeting in 2012, Snap's cofounders, Evan Spiegel and Bobby Murphy, showed that they were building a smartphone app that let users send texts and photos that would quickly disappear. A few other companies were working on something similar, but Evan made me realize that for most of human history, when we talked to each other, the conversation left no record. It couldn't be copied and sent to others or analyzed for advertising—in other words, it wasn't like email, Facebook posts, chats, or tweets. Snapchat would give us a way to have digital communication that would be more like face-to-face conversation, leaving no record. Snap wanted to make technology that would conform to the realities of human nature, while other social media had it the other way around—making humans conform to the unnatural

Context Constantly Changes

way they worked. It was an "Aha!" moment for me. I'm sure it drew on the core learnings that I'd absorbed as a boy, but it came together then: The best products work with human nature, not against it.

Snapchat was also a product of its context. Smartphones with cameras were by then in most people's pockets in advanced countries. Early users of Facebook (founded in 2004) and other social media were getting burned by persistent online images and writings—maybe costing them a job interview or blowing up a relationship. Once we were aware of how Snapchat got context and human nature right, General Catalyst invested. (While Snap started out directionally correct, it lost its North Star along the way—for instance, deciding it was a "camera company" at one point—and hasn't been the transformational company we originally believed in. But it does have a market cap of around $16 billion as of this writing.)

Since my intersection with Snap, context and human nature have been important filters for me and for General Catalyst. It's particularly essential now, as AI swiftly becomes ever more powerful and gets built into almost everything. AI is driving tremendous and accelerating shifts in context. A company that can be built now—like Hippocratic AI—could not have been envisioned a couple of years ago. A year from when you read this, we'll no doubt have AI capabilities that will let us imagine products and services that are inconceivable right now. AI is changing our society. It has and will destroy whole professions yet give rise to new ones. It will help researchers cure cancer, prevent aging, and transform healthcare. It will upend geopolitical balances of power. If done right, AI will be an engine of unprecedented prosperity for every socioeconomic layer. Anyone who is founding or

The Transformation Principles

running a company, investing in companies, or building a career has to be hyperaware of these changes in context and make decisions accordingly.

AI, perhaps more than any technology we've invented, is also a powerful enabler of both the best and worst of human nature. If built and trained improperly, an AI will absorb and turbocharge human biases. Facial-recognition systems can end up discriminating against people of color or helping authoritarian governments track and repress dissenters. Cybersecurity experts are concerned that AI, already able to mimic someone's voice, could be used by hackers to create a mock phone call from your boss asking for passwords to get into the corporate or government computer system. The possibilities for exploiting AI for harmful purposes can seem endless. This is why I've been very cautious about investing in AI that doesn't have a clear purpose of enabling positive change, and why I've encouraged policymakers to help keep AI safe. I founded Responsible Innovation Labs to study the responsible use of AI and recommend best practices.

Yet, perhaps counterintuitively, AI can make us more human. Technologies created over the past 50 years often tended to make us less human—they made us conform to the way they worked, not the other way around. Let's take a simple example: defrosting a chicken breast in a microwave oven. If you do that today, first you have to look up or figure out what setting to use and how much time to punch in. Then you have to find the right buttons and push them in the right order. That's because the microwave can't understand you and has no idea what you're putting into it. You have to act more like a machine than a human so you can instruct the microwave in a language (buttons!) it understands. Now imagine a microwave enabled with AI that can understand

Context Constantly Changes

speech and has been trained on every possible item that could be put inside it. It can also take in information from sensors inside that let the microwave know the weight and dimensions of anything put in there. So, now, you take the rock-hard chicken out of the freezer, put it in the microwave, and speak the simple words, "I need this chicken defrosted." And the microwave knows what you mean, finds the instructions, weighs and measures the chicken, and defrosts it perfectly. If you had a human assistant in the kitchen, that's how you would make the request to that person. You'd just speak the instruction. You'd be a human, not a machine.

AI will move us away from interacting with machines in their language and style and instead allow machines to interact with us like humans. Hippocratic AI is one example. Its AI can hold a humanlike conversation with a user. It is endlessly patient and empathetic, which allows the user to be human and discuss their problems the way they would with another person.

In fact, AI can, in some situations, be more human—appeal more to human nature—than people who get trained and incentivized to act more like machines. In this case, I'm talking about customer contact centers—those places that field your call when you have a problem with a product, or need to change a service, or have a question about a bill. Everyone hates making those calls, because you know you're going to first encounter some frustrating voice-enabled menu to punch through (it's not AI, it's just if-this-then-that software following a script), and then you'll probably get a human who is answering your questions by reading instructions off a screen, and who is doing their best to wrap up the call as quickly as possible. The contact center experience is an offense to human nature. Humans don't communicate through menus and

The Transformation Principles

scripts. We want to have a conversation. We want some empathy. We want to be treated as individuals. But call centers became what they are because of the context in which they were built. Pressure to cut costs pushed businesses to hire call centers—often in countries where labor was cheaper—to handle customers. The automated menus before you get to talk to a person further cut down on labor costs. Instructions on screens cut down on training for operators. The resulting stew of not-great tech and lightly trained people created an unsatisfactory solution for almost everyone involved.

Human nature still craves a human conversation. But now the context has changed with the advances in AI. I invested in a company called Crescendo to take advantage of both the new context and ancient human nature. It was started by Andy Lee, who had previously scaled an enormous (100,000 employees!) contact center company, Alorica, built the old way. He knew it was a flawed experience. It wasn't great for the people calling in, and it wasn't as good as it could be for the businesses Alorica served. Relatively little data was captured from the calls or online interactions, which meant the businesses didn't learn a lot from what customers were asking. Andy and his Crescendo cofounders, Matt Price, Slava Zhakov, and Anand Chandrasekaran, saw a new way to solve these problems by applying AI. "I'm solving a problem that's been driving me crazy for twenty-five years," Andy told me.[27]

Similar to Hippocratic AI's healthcare agents, Crescendo is training AIs on the routines of a contact center and on the customer service details of each of the businesses that contract with Crescendo. For starters, when customers call in by phone, they don't have to first encounter a menu—they get a very humanlike voice that asks questions and understands answers. (In multiple

Context Constantly Changes

languages, without hard-to-understand accents.) "It's very humanlike, and it will only continue to improve," Andy says. From there, the AI agent can be endlessly patient, taking as much time as needed to help the caller, even if it means getting into conversational detours. The AI feels no pressure to quickly resolve the call and get on to the next caller. And the AI agent probably knows more about solving the caller's problem than most human agents would. "When we train a human agent, the retention rate of knowledge is not one hundred percent," Andy says, "and then we have to have continuous training. When we train a machine, it never forgets, so it gives more consistent and accurate answers to customers." The AI can understand tone and intent, discerning when a caller is frustrated or angry. It can, Andy says, be empathetic. For the times when the AI senses it's not able to help the caller, it can send the caller to an actual human expert. "For our initial customers, the results are incredible—depending on the interaction, between sixty and ninety percent can be handled virtually, and the rest get passed on to humans," Andy says. Crescendo has brilliantly played off the tension between changing context and human nature by taking advantage of the AI context shift to give callers a more human experience.

A couple of other notes about Crescendo.

First, because the interactions are through AIs, the AIs are also learning from callers, both to improve their ability to handle interactions and to inform the business about the nature of customer problems and needs. The data goes back to the business so it can fix problems with its product or service or make other changes to improve their customers' experiences.

Second, Andy is aware that the rise of AI call centers could threaten hundreds of thousands of jobs all over the world. But

The Transformation Principles

Andy has an interesting take on that—one that counters the conventional thinking that AI will wipe out jobs. Today, a good many consumers anticipate that an interaction with a contact center will be a frustrating time suck, so they only try it when they've run out of options. But when people realize they can call an AI-driven contact center and each time get a fast and helpful response, they are going to call (or text or email) a lot more—maybe ten times more than they do now. AI will only be able to handle an average of, say, 70% of those calls. That means there will be huge demand for upskilled humans to handle the more challenging calls. "The jobs will become less routine, requiring a high level of knowledge, and they will be more satisfying," Andy says. The work of interacting with customers won't get eliminated, but it will shift to a higher plane.

This is also where General Catalyst can help in a systematic way. We're working to build other companies, such as Guild and Multiverse, that are reinventing the way workers learn and develop new career paths. Keep in mind that while AI will make some jobs for humans obsolete, it will also be able to scale very humanlike and inexpensive one-on-one coaching. Learning new skills will be more accessible to more people than ever before. The goal is to ultimately help people have more rewarding lives, not less rewarding.

This push to make machines more human is the mission for Applied Intuition too. Today, you get in a Tesla and, as smart as it is, you have to figure out which buttons to push on a complicated screen just to turn on the heat or navigate to a location. Before long, your new-model intelligent car will interact with you on a human level. You'll just say, "It's cold in here!" and the heat will come on. You'll be able to ask the car to do whatever you want

Context Constantly Changes

the car to do. Once cars can fully drive themselves, you'll get in and talk to it the way you would a human driver: "I want to go to Costco but need to stop by my sister's house on the way." The car will understand.

This principle of *context constantly changes but human nature stays the same* is a crucial guide when our company invests in AI-driven transformation. It's also important to the way we work with founders and to the kinds of founders we want to work with.

It is human nature to prioritize short-term rewards over long-term goals. It's why a student skips a morning class and sleeps in even if it hurts his or her ability to graduate, or why that bowl of ice cream is so tempting when the goal is to lose weight. Founders and CEOs are not immune to short-term temptations when running their companies. One result of that has been the "move fast and break things" mentality in the tech ecosystem—a mentality that usually doesn't include thinking through what to do once things are broken. To be a founder or leader of an enduring company, you need to balance short-term rewards with long-term strategy. Great founders understand their own human nature and have the discipline to overcome it when necessary. As investors, we seek out those founders, but we also understand they are human. So we've built a culture at General Catalyst that encourages our founders to focus on the long term and rewards them for it. Our focus on building enduring, responsible companies that have a positive impact creates a support system for long-term thinking. All the signals around our ecosystem point away from "move fast and break things" and toward responsible, impactful innovation.

And as a driver of innovation and transformation, we believe we have to be hyperaware of what AI can do now and what it will be able to do soon and of how the context around AI is being

The Transformation Principles

shaped—including laws that will regulate it, societal backlash or fears that might slow its acceptance, and rifts among nations that might result in different versions of AI in different regions.

It's why we have taken the stance that AI should be open source, not controlled by a few giant corporations that will, in all likelihood, use it to further their own interests. And AI needs responsible guardrails. Policymakers and our industry must embrace the fact that bad people will want to do bad things with AI, and the more that happens, the more governments and society will push to slow AI's progress. It's a delicate balance to make sure AI works for us and not against us. It can't be left to run wild, yet we don't want governments to keep AI from developing. We've seen this situation before after splitting the atom. The technology could be made to produce nuclear bombs or nuclear energy. The one thing society couldn't risk was letting any nation or person get hold of the technology, so the world set up mechanisms to restrict it. Unfortunately, those restrictions ended up being so tight that, as a planet, we largely failed to harness nuclear technology for energy. Otherwise, we might have less of a climate crisis today. Let's not make that same mistake with AI and waste this opportunity.

General Catalyst's mission to reinvent healthcare has been heavily influenced by this principle about context and human nature, including the ability of AI to help us feel more human.

First of all, the traditional fee-for-service healthcare system is an insult to human nature. It is in our nature to want to stay healthy, active, and vibrant—the lowest rung on the hierarchy of needs and essential to success and happiness. Yet traditional

Context Constantly Changes

healthcare is not set up to keep us healthy, active, and vibrant—it is set up to treat us once we're sick. That's how the system makes money, which means the system is incentivized to let you get sick so it can get paid to fix you. And even then, the system forces you to navigate it, making you conform to how it works. You have to find doctors on your own, go through the inconvenience of going to their offices even though you're sick, coordinate your own care, manage insurance—everyone is familiar with the nightmare of healthcare.

Any system that creates so much friction with human nature is ripe for reinvention. We all—even those who work in healthcare—want a system designed to keep us healthy. We want a health assurance system that understands each of our individual health situations and takes care of us in a way that conforms to our lives, as if each of us has our own personal doctor constantly monitoring our health and caring for us. But to begin to truly change traditional healthcare into the more human-centered health assurance, we needed help from a big change in context. Cue the recent arrival of superpowerful AI.

I started to see the possibilities of reinventing healthcare when Glen Tullman and I built Livongo. We began by acknowledging human nature. As mentioned before, it's human nature to stay healthy, not get sick—but the US healthcare system is set up, and economically incentivized, to treat people after they get sick. And it's human nature to prioritize short-term rewards over long-term health, so in order to keep people healthy, we need a system that helps people overcome problematic short-term decisions.

With that in mind, we knew that the healthcare system treats everyone with diabetes pretty much the same, even though every person's condition is unique. So, we felt there was a need

The Transformation Principles

for technology that would learn about the health of each individual diabetes patient and guide them so their condition would have as little impact on their lives as possible. Our driving insight was: People who have diabetes don't want to think about their diabetes.

When we founded Livongo in 2008, AI wasn't what it is now. As we navigated ambiguity toward the future we wanted to create, Livongo became a combination of AI, cloud, mobile, and human intervention. It worked, and inspired us to believe that all of healthcare should use technology to keep us healthy and out of doctors' offices and hospitals. We founded or invested in other companies that can help make that reinvention happen—companies such as Commure, Homeward, Cityblock, and Hippocratic AI. In keeping with the transformation principles, we have understood that healthcare is an enormous and complex sector that no single company can change by itself. The way to reinvent it is to collaborate with the existing system, prove out new technologies and approaches, change mindsets, and work with policymakers to help nourish and shape a new future for our health.

One more point about human nature and context as it applies to healthcare and, in this case, crypto. As noted, I avoided investing in crypto in its early years because I believed its killer app was greed. Instead of driving powerful positive change, cryptocurrencies played to our worst temptations. But I also recognized that blockchain-based crypto, divorced from treating it like easy money, is a powerful technology. It just needed to be used in the right context and be responsible about human nature. That realization led us to help launch a company in 2023 called HealthEx, cofounded by Priyanka Agarwal and Anand Raghavan.

Context Constantly Changes

Priyanka is a physician who spent much of her career in academic medicine and the biotech/life sciences spaces. High-quality data is critical to more efficiently studying rare diseases, but it can be hard to come by. Such diseases affect such a small segment of the population. Priyanka started thinking there must be a way to get better data directly from the source—from patients and the health systems who manage their data. She wanted to set up a mechanism that would incentivize patients to participate while protecting their privacy. Her solution is an ecosystem based on blockchain systems that give participants a way to control their data and see how it is being used.

Let's say you're a patient—especially a patient with a less-common condition—and you'd like to help researchers and innovators find cures and treatments or develop AI models to support clinical care. HealthEx gives you an easy and safe way to do that. When you onboard with the health system caring for you, you indicate your interest in participating. Your medical records can be accessed by researchers or innovators, and the software looks for matches between your condition and efforts to find new treatments for it—such as a clinical trial for a drug, work on a new medical device, or access by a team looking to develop AI models from patients like you. You get notified and can decide whether to participate and what data you'll consent to release. The researchers only get to see the data you consent to show them. And you get some value in return. Researchers and innovators can offer to pay for your information and participation, and this value goes to the health system and you as the patient. All of this works in a similar way as cryptocurrencies.

HealthEx could be a game-changer for medical researchers and innovators. The more data they can work with, the more

The Transformation Principles

likely they can get to a good outcome and get there more quickly, and that translates into lives saved and patients getting relief from their conditions. Until now, getting patient data has been a mostly manual process: Researchers would have to contact a health system, tell them what they were looking for, and then the health system would have to look up records to find the right patients and call each one to ask about participation. (Once agreeing, the patient would have little visibility into what data gets shared or how it's being used.) With HealthEx, the researchers and innovators can plug in the patients they're looking for. The system comes back with matches and can automatically reach out to those patients. Once a pool of patients agrees to join in, the system enforces the data-sharing preferences of each patient. The blockchain-based system for data auditing ensures that payment and data-licensing opportunities are tied to data access.

All in all, HealthEx gives patients and health systems an easy way to boost research and innovation that might help them, with data safety and transparency built in, plus a way to layer on more interesting data licensing models for sharing data.

HealthEx is still in its early stages and as of this writing is gearing up for its first set of deployments at leading health systems. "Our thinking is that HealthEx is quite aspirational," Priyanka says. "It will take time. It's a journey. But if this works, the possibilities from a research perspective are huge." It could lead to one breakthrough after another for curing rare but devastating diseases.[28]

It's human nature to want to contribute to something positive that is bigger than ourselves. It is human nature to want control over something valuable that belongs to us—in this case, information about our health. It is human nature to want to help cure

Context Constantly Changes

a disease that might kill us. Priyanka believes she is getting the right human-nature incentives lined up to make this work while keeping at bay the aspects of crypto that can tempt bad behavior. Context has changed, giving us a technology and mechanism that can help positively tap into the constants of human nature to do something good.

CHAPTER EIGHT

THE CHOICE BETWEEN POSITIVE IMPACT AND RETURNS IS FALSE

Siva Yellamraju grew up in India, studied engineering, moved to the United States after college, and started multiple tech companies. He sold one to Google and another to Apple. While his companies helped make our devices and apps work better, even Siva would be hard-pressed to say they had a powerful positive impact on society. The businesses generated good returns but not outsized long-term returns.

When thinking about what to do next, Siva, along with cofounder Ali-Amir Aldan, wanted both positive impact and compounding returns, understanding that these things are not mutually exclusive but in fact go together.

He studied climate change, looking for a technology that would have the potential to make a major difference. "That's when I bumped into hydrogen," Siva says. "I spent a good year focusing on this problem. It was a very different landscape for me. I spent a lot of time visiting chemical factories across the globe."[29]

Hydrogen as a fuel has a lot of advantages. It burns clean. It's abundant—it can be made from water. It's not toxic. But it

The Transformation Principles

has so far failed to really work as a replacement for fossil fuels. Instead, fossil fuels have had to be burned to make hydrogen, and that process would happen in a centralized facility, so the hydrogen would have to be shipped to end users in gasoline-powered tanker trucks—all of which defeats the purpose, which is to reduce greenhouse gas emissions. Over the past 15 years, new solid-membrane technologies have been invented that can more efficiently break water into hydrogen and oxygen. Yet, still, hydrogen hasn't become a viable replacement for fossil fuels.

But Siva hit on an idea that changed his approach: Hydrogen isn't a fuel—it's a battery. One of the problems with renewable energy like solar and wind is that it is not steadily, predictably produced. Solar produces energy when it's sunny; wind when it's windy. To be effective as an energy source, the energy has to be stored for those times when it's not sunny or windy. That takes batteries, but typical batteries have challenging issues. Battery storage is relatively short term. It's not good for, say, powering heavy equipment or machinery that has to operate around the clock. A battery degrades when cold. It is an environmental hazard when discarded.

Siva and Ali-Amir cofounded a company, Fourier, to develop membrane technology, driven by sophisticated software, that can turn water into hydrogen using renewable energy. And it will do this with machinery operating at the end user's site. Set up the device, connect it to a water source, and it can make hydrogen on demand, ready for use as power whenever it's needed. "We want to make on-site hydrogen production universally accessible—large or small, scaled up or down in an efficient way," Siva says.

As of this writing, Fourier is still building prototypes and testing. If it succeeds in developing a new category of small-scale,

The Choice Between Positive Impact and Returns

efficient, on-demand hydrogen generators, it stands a chance of becoming an important and monumentally valuable company. By finding a solution to a hard problem that matters to society, Fourier can reduce the harm of carbon emissions while generating great long-term returns. When I met Siva, he wasn't even looking to raise capital. But General Catalyst lobbied to join with Fourier because the company met our principle: The choice between positive impact and returns is false. In fact, positive impact is the key to generating the best returns.

Here's another climate-related story, this one about an entrepreneur who is very much a capitalist interested in making money and finding a way to do that while also making a positive impact with massive potential. Peter Reinhardt, once a student of mine at MIT, was the founder of an enterprise data company called Segment, and in 2020 he sold it to Twilio for $3.2 billion. Around the same time, Reinhardt started another company, Charm Industrial, which is now a pioneer in a technology called "bio-oil sequestration." Charm takes agricultural residue and wildfire fuel load biomass, both of which would ordinarily release carbon into the atmosphere as they decay or burn, and converts it to a substance that's similar to the liquid smoke used in barbecue sauce. But it's not food grade or useful for anything else. Charm then injects that bad oil back into the ground, preventing it from adding to climate change.

It's a business because, increasingly, companies either have to or want to work toward having a zero-carbon footprint, getting rid of as much or more carbon from the atmosphere as they put in. So Charm sells carbon removal credits to corporate buyers. Those corporations are essentially paying Charm to get rid of carbon for them. As regulations force more companies to reduce carbon,

The Transformation Principles

carbon removal will become a multibillion-dollar annual industry. Peter tells me that as Charm scales its technology, it will become one of the lowest-cost ways to remove carbon, and it will still be a very profitable business. "That seems pretty concrete at this point," Peter says. Online payments company Stripe, for example, is a Charm customer. A company like Stripe doesn't have a way to capture its own carbon emissions and bury them. Instead, Stripe can turn to Charm, buy an amount of carbon from other sources that are equivalent to Stripe's emissions, and then have Charm turn it into permanently buried oil. Everyone wins: Stripe makes good on its carbon pledge; the world winds up with less carbon in the atmosphere; and Charm makes a profit so it can continue to develop the technology.[30]

Charm also commissioned an economic study, which showed that their planned activities would create 20,000 direct and indirect jobs—most of them in the American heartland—and add two billion dollars to the US gross domestic product (GDP) by 2030—and potentially 200,000 jobs by 2040.[31]

In 1970, economist Milton Friedman published an essay that scolded business leaders for getting involved in that era's roiling social and political issues. He wrote that "social responsibility" is not a business's concern, and that a company's responsibility is only to increase profits and shareholder value. Social issues should be something that individuals, political parties, and nonprofits work on. Over the next 50 years, Friedman's point of view settled in as the accepted wisdom in business: Companies exist for one reason, and that is to increase shareholder value. Generations

The Choice Between Positive Impact and Returns

of business leaders have believed that there is a choice between positive impact and returns, and their only focus should be on returns.

But that choice has always been false—it is now, and it was in Friedman's era.

What Friedman and business leaders have often missed is that "positive impact" changes with the times. In the twentieth century, as populations exploded, we needed companies to scale up society. That meant creating jobs and a middle class, building homes and cities, making food plentiful and affordable, making the masses healthy and safe. Over the course of a century, all of these achievements—lifting much of society out of poverty and giving us purpose, security, and health—nearly doubled life expectancy in advanced nations. That is one of the greatest triumphs in human history. And companies that contributed, from Procter & Gamble to Nestlé, Merck, General Motors, IBM, and General Electric, also generated outsized returns over long stretches of time. Society rewarded such companies because those companies made society better.

But society has different needs now. Populations of many developed countries are shrinking. Much of last century's scaling up relied on burning fossil fuels, but because of that, now we're in a climate crisis. Healthcare systems made more people healthy yet have grown so complex and disconnected from their customers that healthcare is now a terrible experience and financial burden. Technology is being used to tear the fabric of the society we built last century. Social media and misinformation have fueled political and social divides. Online retail and remote work are hollowing out city centers. Automation, software, and, now, powerful AI are eating jobs and whole professions. Much of the wealth that tech creates goes to the educated upper classes, contributing to wider and wider wealth gaps.

Going forward, "positive impact" means addressing these newer issues. Just as we once needed profit-making businesses to help society by scaling up infrastructure and a middle class, we now need profit-making businesses to help society address climate change, divides, healthcare, and a reinvention of work, among other critical problems. Such companies—as with Fourier—are often hard to build. But they are the companies that will generate the greatest long-term returns. They will be the next P&Gs, Mercks, IBMs, and GEs.

Companies thrive when they operate in the best interests of society. You can build a business and monetize it in the short term and not worry about whether it's good for society, and maybe you sell it to Apple or Google like Siva did. That can be enough for some entrepreneurs. But it's not the best long-term strategy. Society won't let a business prosper and generate compounding returns if it's not good for society. (Look what happened to tobacco companies once society turned on them.)

How does this principle fit with the extreme success of today's tech behemoths: Microsoft, Alphabet (formerly Google), Apple, Amazon, Meta, and, most recently, Nvidia?

Society has legitimate concerns about the monopolistic power of these companies, and certainly their success has had some problematic consequences. Google's success contributed to the evisceration of journalism in the United States. Amazon's success contributed to closed retail shops across the country. Meta may have been the most problematic as it was used to spread misinformation and fake news while also adding to the crisis in legitimate journalism.

The Choice Between Positive Impact and Returns

Yet in many substantial ways, these companies got so enormous and generated such outsized returns because they positively impacted society. It's hard to imagine life today without Alphabet's Google search, Maps, Gmail, and YouTube. Apple created a mobile device platform that revolutionized the way we live and work—again, hard to imagine life without iPhones and the many Android models that mimicked Apple's model. Amazon created consumer convenience that we'll never want to give up, and it proved to be a critical lifeline when the world shut down during the 2020–2021 pandemic. Nvidia developed the chips that make today's AI possible, opening the way for a new generation of AI-driven companies that—with the right principles—will further benefit society.

Meta and Microsoft are interesting when looked at through this lens of impact plus returns. In my view, Meta's returns to shareholders got tamped down through the late 2010s, during a time when many saw Meta's Facebook and Instagram as platforms that were harming society—particularly spreading misinformation and hate speech and contributing to mental health issues among teenagers—while CEO Mark Zuckerberg seemed tone-deaf to the issues. In 2023, as Zuckerberg and the company seemed to embrace a more responsible attitude, Meta shares rose sharply. Microsoft's returns completely stalled throughout Steve Ballmer's tenure as CEO from 2000 to 2014. In my view, that was because Ballmer tried to make Microsoft into a consumer company, introducing products like the Zune music player, Microsoft smartphones, and the Bing search engine—all of which copied more successful products (iPod, iPhone, Google) already on the market. Microsoft in those years didn't necessarily have a negative impact, but it also didn't contribute much of anything to

The Transformation Principles

society that we needed. Its impact was just kind of meh. Microsoft's share price was almost exactly the same on the day Ballmer took over and the day he handed the CEO job to Satya Nadella 14 years later. Satya then remade Microsoft into a digital picks-and-shovels business—operating systems, productivity software, cloud computing, AI—that has become an important platform for innovation. It may not be sexy, but Microsoft is contributing technology that society needs. Since Satya took over, Microsoft's value has grown by nearly ten times. Once Microsoft was generating positive impact, the returns rocketed.

What does all this mean for investors and founders?

First, positive impact drives enduring returns. If you want to build a company that thrives for generations, find a hard problem that society needs to address and help fix it. Use powerful new technologies we're creating, such as AI, blockchain, gene editing and others, to rethink and reinvent outdated sectors that no longer work in the best interests of society—sectors like healthcare, transportation, banking, and energy.

The flip side is that we need profitable, capitalistic, return-generating companies to achieve positive impact. Capitalism, guided by responsible innovation, is the most effective mechanism we have for powerful positive change. In every way, the idea that positive impact vs. returns is a choice to be made is false. Impact plus positive returns is a necessary combination to embrace.

There is a second part to this principle, as detailed above: The meaning of "positive impact" changes with the times. For example, in one era it seemed like industry was driving positive impact for

The Choice Between Positive Impact and Returns

society by manufacturing gas-powered cars and drilling for oil. Today, that has become a negative impact, and companies that rely on those businesses are in decline. (ExxonMobil stock has all but stalled since 2007. General Motors shares, adjusted for inflation, are a fraction of their peak in the 1960s.) Positive impact now means finding ways to operate society on clean, renewable energy.

Across every aspect of society, positive impact likely means something different today than it would have a couple of decades ago. So, a company has to get it right on the positive impact side of the equation. Then it's all about execution to succeed and generate enduring returns.

I came to this principle later in my life. For the first decade of my venture capital career, I invested in good companies that met at least some of the previous principles. When Ken Chenault, the former American Express CEO, joined General Catalyst, he helped me understand the connection between positive impact and enduring returns.

American Express has thrived for more than a century because it has continuously reinvented itself in ways that have had a positive impact through changing times. Merck has also prospered for more than one hundred years for similar reasons. Its former CEO, Ken Frazier, is now on our team, and he has reinforced what I've learned from Ken Chenault. The companies that I have long admired most are the ones that have prospered for more than a century by constantly creating positive impact for their times—companies such as Unilever, IBM, and Corning.

Our adventure with Livongo, though, convinced me that

The Transformation Principles

traditional venture capital is not structured to drive long-term transformation, which means VC is not structured to capture the returns generated because of positive impact.

Venture capital is a proven engine of innovation. It gets new companies and technologies off the ground and into the market. And then, because of the nature of VC funds and expectations of limited partners, VCs look for an exit—a way to capture the value of their gains and distribute it to the limited partners. That exit is usually an IPO or selling the startup to a larger company, and it typically marks the end of the VC's involvement. In the case of Livongo, General Catalyst cofounded the company, funded it, and helped guide it as it worked on its innovative approach to helping patients manage their diabetes. By 2020, about six years after it was founded, Livongo was serving 500,000 patients, and then Teledoc bought it for $18 billion.

But if our mission was to drive positive impact for the long run and reap the returns, we failed. We reached a fraction of the 30 million Americans with diabetes. If General Catalyst had a mechanism for holding on to and guiding Livongo until it completely reinvented diabetes treatment, our returns would have been multiples of that $18 billion. We would've had greater impact and made far more money.

This was my "Aha!" moment. I want to be able to play the long game, because that's the way to maximize impact and returns. That's why we're developing a new kind of entity, which I have been describing throughout this book. General Catalyst will still have its venture capital group at the core. That will continue to be our engine of innovation. But we have to marry it to a part of General Catalyst that becomes an engine of transformation. It will operate on a different business model that allows for longer

The Choice Between Positive Impact and Returns

time horizons and more involvement in operations. When a company comes up through the VC arm and shows, like Livongo, that it can have an important positive impact, we'll have a mechanism for holding on to our share of the company, driving that impact, and enjoying compounding and enduring returns. Some of those returns can then be reinvested into the venture capital engine of innovation, giving us a flywheel effect.

At a meta level, our goal is to have a positive impact on the venture capital industry, influencing it to think beyond "exit" to "endurance." We want General Catalyst to prove that enduring positive impact leads to the best returns, because if we prove that's true, others will follow.

At the least, it is in our soul to pursue impact plus returns. We believe it's the future of innovation and transformation. As happens when an entity has a strong soul, we will work until we find the best way to drive impact plus returns and end the mindset that there is a choice between impact and returns.

This principle, like all the others, guides our choices at General Catalyst. In particular, it drives us to focus on industries that are no longer operating in society's best interests. These are industries where we can have a powerful positive impact. But we're not focusing on such industries because we're benevolent philanthropists. We are capitalists. We believe that the best way for us to generate compounding returns is to have a positive impact on society—and we believe that the more effective way to impact society is through profitable capitalism. This is how the goals of society and capitalism align.

The Transformation Principles

It is why we started with healthcare. The more I got involved with the sector, at first through Humedica and then Livongo, the more I comprehended how badly it is misaligned with the people it's meant to help. Healthcare is in need of positive change. Even those who work in healthcare believe that. It is a sector that everyone has to deal with at one time or another—we and our loved ones eventually need medical help. We want to invest in technologies that change the nature of healthcare so the system conforms to the patient and the goal is to keep people healthy, not just treat them once they're sick. If we can demonstrate in healthcare that positive change leads to great enduring returns, it gives us permission to dive into the same transformation process in other sectors such as energy and banking.

In healthcare, our venture arm funds innovations that we believe will contribute to positive change. As those innovations come to fruition, we look at the company through the lens of the transformation principles: Are the founders creating a new future; are they navigating ambiguity; do they have a collaborative mindset? If the answer to those questions is no, we will look to exit. If yes, we can bring them into our longer-term engine of transformation.

As I write this, we're building that engine of transformation—our first one. As outlined in earlier chapters, the healthcare engine of transformation includes a consortium of more than two dozen hospital systems and the Ohio health system, Summa Health, that General Catalyst is buying outright. Buying a hospital is materially different from anything any VC has ever done. It's also a different path than any hospital system has ever taken. It's more common for a hospital to be bought by a private equity group, which then cuts costs to try to improve margins and

The Choice Between Positive Impact and Returns

wring as much cash out of the acquisition as possible. That's adamantly *not* our intention. Our plan is to invest in new technologies and processes that will make Summa Health even better for its community, helping us prove to the healthcare sector that there are better ways to run hospital systems so people stay healthier, healthcare professionals do more rewarding work, and outcomes for everyone improve. Instead of taking costs out, the goal is to put innovation in. Again, this aligns with our principle that profit and impact go hand in hand.

Our venture group will continue to fund and found tech companies that, like Livongo, help reinvent the way people take care of their health. But to truly reinvent healthcare will require a constellation of companies and new technologies—and their adoption and acceptance by doctors, nurses, administrators, insurers, and others in the system. The hospital systems that collaborate with us can give innovations a fertile place to prove themselves, grow, and mature. The startups that create innovations that have a powerful positive impact will find traction and help healthcare systems reinvent themselves. Those startups become megasuccesses, generating enduring returns. The healthcare systems become better at keeping their populations healthy and giving them a healthcare experience that's more human. Society overall gets a healthier population at a lower cost. Everyone benefits, and the returns get cycled back to finance new innovations to keep the cycle going.

Imagine if every venture capital firm married an engine of innovation to an engine of transformation, all of them contributing to the reinvention of industries that are stuck in the past and harming society.

Imagine if that helps prove to every investor, founder, CEO,

The Transformation Principles

and policymaker that powerful positive impact leads to great returns, and great returns create more positive impact. Our society would make capitalism work for the greater good and leave the Friedman philosophy in the dust.

Proving that this is right is our goal at General Catalyst.

CHAPTER NINE

THE BEST RESULTS COME FROM LEADING WITH CURIOSITY AND GENEROSITY

I was an early investor in Stripe. It turned out to be the most important investment I ever made. Of course, Stripe has been a fabulous success, and our multiple rounds of investment in the company have generated immense returns. But there's another reason this has been important to me. Despite his relatively young age, Stripe cofounder and CEO Patrick Collison has continuously inspired me with his leadership style. He has helped me fully understand the principle: The best results come from leading with curiosity and generosity.

I try to live by this principle as a leader at General Catalyst, and I also look for that in the company founders that come through our doors.

Curious leaders know they don't know everything or have all the answers. They perpetually seek out learning. They listen to others. Their mindset is in keeping with having a beginner's mind—with looking at every problem with an innocence about what can or can't be done.

Generous leaders build up and support their followers, making

The Transformation Principles

them better. They work to achieve win-win with employees, partners, suppliers, investors, and every other stakeholder. They seek to see and avoid unintended negative consequences of products they build and instead contribute positively to the world.

I see all of that in Patrick.

Patrick and his brother John grew up in a rural Irish village called Dromineer. You could label them prodigies. When Patrick was 16, he won Ireland's young scientist of the year award for building a conversational AI using the Lisp programming language. At 17, he and John, who was then 15, launched their first startup, Auctomatic, which helped eBay sellers track their inventory. Patrick got into MIT, where I first met him. John got into Harvard. They sold Auctomatic in 2008 for five million dollars. Patrick was 19 and John was 17.

They were interested in e-commerce and cloud software, and they quickly found out that while it was easy then to sell products online, collecting payments was hard—even harder when selling across national borders. The brothers went looking for something like what Stripe does but couldn't find it, so they started Stripe in 2009. They built a system that made it super simple for anyone to collect online payments. They were passionate about expanding opportunities for people online—a mission that later coalesced into Stripe's mission of "increasing the GDP of the internet." That mission was in their soul; they were playing their own game; they were creating a new future for entrepreneurs. I didn't know exactly where they were going with Stripe, but I knew I saw something in Patrick and John and believed they were onto something.

In 2024, as I write this, around three million websites and cloud entities use Stripe for payments, and it processes more than one trillion dollars in payments a year. Stripe has become

The Best Results Come from Leading with Curiosity

integral to the tech ecosystem, and it still has immense potential for growth.

Patrick has proven to be a leader worth emulating. I haven't met many people who are so voraciously curious. He is well-known as a bookaholic and regularly writes about the books he's been reading. If you go to his house, books are piled up everywhere. His curiosity is endless. He's often told me that there are so many things he feels he should know but doesn't, and he soaks up books and information to try to solve that.

In another sign of curiosity (and humility), I've seen how Patrick randomly reaches out to people whose work he admires—academics, business leaders, writers, artists—hoping to learn from them. Some of those contacts have turned into friendships, like with well-known economist Tyler Cowen. It's striking how Patrick listens. When someone holds a point of view that's different from his, he tries not to do the natural thing, which is to lock in on why that person is wrong. He tries to figure out if they might be right. Or at least why they believe they're right.

As for being a generous leader, Patrick truly cares about making all of the internet better. Stripe has expanded beyond payments to create a suite of products that make it easier to set up all of the back end of an online business. Stripe launched a book publishing arm—a by-product of Patrick's love of books—to publish books that help startups operate better. Stripe Press published Elad Gil's influential *High Growth Handbook*. To Patrick, Stripe's role in online commerce is about making the whole world better and more equal. He wants to help entrepreneurs in developing countries compete online with anyone from anywhere.

This is the way Patrick thinks and acts. And when hiring, he looks to hire other curious and generous leaders. Sure, Stripe looks for the best and brightest, but, as Patrick often says, the company seeks to find people who have interpersonal warmth and a desire to make others around them better.

Of course, Patrick isn't the only curious and generous leader in business—he just happens to be one I know well. I've been lucky enough to have Ken Chenault as my mentor, and I consider him another person who leads with curiosity and generosity. Ken Frazier and Marc Harrison both had amazing careers leading with curiosity and generosity, and now I also get to work with and learn from them at General Catalyst. For his bestselling book *Good to Great*, Jim Collins used a massive data set to identify companies that transformed themselves after decades of existence, and then he identified the traits of the leaders who pulled off these good-to-great transformations. Such leaders—Collins called them "Level 5 leaders"—tend to fit the mold of "curious and generous." The five characteristics Collins found are common in Level 5 leaders are humility, self-awareness, a strong sense of purpose, a desire for continuous learning, and a determination to do what's right, not what's easy.

Such curiosity and generosity are traits of founders I want to back and work with. Founders like that are the most likely to build companies that combine powerful positive impact with compounding returns.

In Hindu culture, people sometimes turn to a swami for spiritual guidance and moral support. A swami is something like a priest or a monk in Christianity or a rabbi in Judaism, though perhaps less focused on religion and more attuned to helping people in

The Best Results Come from Leading with Curiosity

their pursuit of self-actualization and enlightenment. My mother has a swami, and about a decade before writing this book, he and I went for a walk, and I asked him, "What is the purpose of life?" He answered: "To be happy." I asked him what "being happy" means, and he turned it back on me, saying what matters is what being happy means to me.

I thought about this for a year before I had an answer. A key was thinking about my always-crammed calendar and what entries give me energy versus those that sap my energy. The meetings and phone calls in which I'm helping someone or learning something give me energy, and those situations make me happy. Since then, when filling my calendar, I've tried to maximize the time dedicated to learning and helping. In situations where it might not be obvious how to learn or help, I now look for a way to do one or the other or both. That has made me happier in life and helps fulfill my sense of purpose.

If you are always learning and have a servant-leader mindset, I believe you will have a more fulfilling life, be a better leader, and get better results. That applies to an individual but also should inform the culture of an organization or a society. Curious and generous leaders build cultures that breed diversity of thought and embrace sound principles. They activate people and get them to be their best. They create movements that are bigger than themselves. If this kind of mindset would prevail, we wouldn't have capitalism that is rapacious and lopsided, benefiting the 1% while leaving others behind. We'd have inclusive capitalism, with businesses focused on creating an equitable society and fixing hard problems—impact plus returns.

It's not just my theory. The results of leading with curiosity and generosity are tangible. Ken Chenault, who influenced my

The Transformation Principles

thinking about curious and generous leadership, led American Express from 2001 to 2018. During that time, annual profits rose from $1.3 billion to $5.3 billion, revenue doubled, and the stock doubled. When Ken left Amex, Warren Buffett was quoted saying, "His record is really hard to match in corporate America."

One of the best-known proponents of curious and generous leadership was the late Herb Kelleher, who started Southwest Airlines in 1971 as a low-fare airline flying from Dallas to Houston and San Antonio. He preached servant leadership from the beginning. "I have always believed that the best leader is the best server," Kelleher once said. "And if you're a servant, by definition, you're not controlling. We try to value each person individually and to be cognizant of them as human beings—not just people who work for our company."[32] He also noted: "Your employees come first. There's no question about that. If your employees are satisfied and happy and dedicated and inspired by what they are doing, then they make your customers happy and they come back. And that makes your shareholders happy." When Kelleher stepped down in 2008, Southwest had been profitable for 36 consecutive years, a record in the commercial airline industry. Its 2008 profits were $178 million. *The New York Times* reported that at the annual meeting when Kelleher stepped down, he received "the kind of standing ovation usually reserved for rock stars."[33] The Southwest pilots union took out full-page newspaper ads thanking him for all he'd done.

In a 2023 study, academic researchers led by James Lemoine at the University at Buffalo School of Management scored companies on servant leadership. They concluded that at companies with a servant leadership culture, employees tended to think through

The Best Results Come from Leading with Curiosity

problems and find creative solutions. A one-point increase in a company's servant leadership score (on a seven-point scale) correlated to a 6% increase in revenue.[34]

Certainly, there are leaders who succeed who are not curious or generous but instead are tyrannical or narcissistic. I'm not willing to bet on those types of leaders. The odds are against them in the long run, and I'm interested in building companies that endure and generate compounding returns. A tyrannical founder may show me amazing technology that could solve an important problem, but I find it hard to believe such a person can build an enduring company and culture that has a long-term positive impact. A founder might come to General Catalyst meeting many of the previous principles, but if they can't find it in them to lead with curiosity and generosity, I will pass.

I strive to be a curious and generous leader at General Catalyst and at the companies where I play a leadership role. As you've read in this book, it's important to me to maintain a beginner's mind, which sometimes means getting involved in industries I know little about. I try to be aware of how much I don't know. That awareness drives me to seek teachers. I constantly reach out to people in many different fields—business leaders, politicians, authors, scientists, doctors—and ask for their guidance. In my position as a CEO, board member, or venture capitalist, people often seem to think I always have the answers and then are caught off guard when I ask, "What do you think?" The question is sincere. I want to know.

As a day-to-day manager of people, my Hindu upbringing

informs my leadership style. It helps that I believe that this lifetime is but one stop on a much longer journey. That belief makes momentary disappointments and victories seem less weighty. That in turn helps me manage my emotions. When things go wrong, instead of getting angry, I seek to understand why, and I ask for help trying to fix it. When things go right, I give credit to those who helped make that happen, and I ask them to do more because I believe in their ability to do more. Though I have often been in the news or on stage, believe me, it's not because I seek attention—it's in service of General Catalyst and our goals. As I've noted, I want General Catalyst to be on a journey through many lives and generations. I remind myself constantly that I am in service of building something bigger than myself.

Leading with curiosity and generosity links to what General Catalyst chooses to work on and the companies we start or fund. We believe inclusive capitalism—a generous version of capitalism that intentionally lifts up everyone—is much like servant leadership. The more a business positively impacts the world, the better that business's chances of generating great, enduring returns. When someone builds a business that benefits only a thin slice of society and focuses solely on profits and only later turns to philanthropy to give away billions—that's seeking atonement, not practicing generosity. Leading with generosity means building a business that positively impacts society with the products it makes and the way it behaves throughout its existence.

I often remind my team when they're negotiating or working on a new deal to focus on what really matters. Because our industry is one where the small stuff rarely does. The best companies I've invested in were not perfect from the outset—they learned and grew over time, usually in accordance with the principles in

The Best Results Come from Leading with Curiosity

this book. We're playing the long game here, and people want to work with those who are curious and generous.

That applies inside of GC, too, as illustrated by the story of Pranav Singhvi. Pranav grew up in Abu Dhabi, went to college in the United States, and landed at Palantir Technologies, running the strategic finance team. He joined General Catalyst in 2019, and he came with some intriguing questions about how technology companies deploy capital for growth. He shared his ideas with me, and, in accordance with our culture of curiosity, I let him explore his theories.

Pranav dug into the data and had conversations with founders and investors and eventually came to an intriguing conclusion: Once a company reaches a certain size, in order to scale it has to invest capital in sales and marketing—and the investment in sales and marketing produces a reasonably predictable return. So, why don't companies use traditional debt to fund this investment? The reason is that debt has to be paid back regardless of the return generated by sales and marketing—in a time frame that has nothing to do with the return on sales and marketing. This adds substantial risk to the business.

As a result, founders often raise or reinvest their equity to fund sales and marketing, which, as Pranav says, "is actually not a great use of capital." Pranav wondered if General Catalyst could invest just in a company's sales and marketing and get paid back from the gross profit generated by the sales and marketing that General Catalyst funded, up to a capped return. That would mean the company would not add risk on the downside and not have to give up equity upside. For GC, it's a very different model from investing to get equity or traditional debt.[35]

"The pitch to founders is: Once you reach product/market fit

The Transformation Principles

and are spending at least one million dollars a month on sales and marketing—today you're spending your own money," Pranav says. "What if we funded a percentage of that, and will only get paid when it works up to a capped return. You can then spend your excess capital to build products, for engineering, for acquisitions and so on."

I let Pranav start it as a side project. I actually told him I thought it was never going to work. But he proved me wrong. Founders love it and the returns for us have been meaningful. Superplay, a gaming company, was able to use Pranav's program to grow its customer base while raising only $50 million in equity capital, which the company spent largely on product and engineering instead of sales and marketing. In 2024, Superplay was acquired by Playtika for two billion dollars.

Now Pranav runs what we call the "Customer Value Fund." It has invested in more than 40 companies and is deploying more than $100 million a month.

All because we ran with his curiosity.

We are hyperaware that we found and back companies that are developing AI products and services that will shift or eliminate some types of jobs. We cannot be generous leaders, or proponents of inclusive capitalism, and ignore that fact. Workforce transformation and training must be a part of what we do. As some companies automate jobs, we need others to create new ones, ultimately creating more work, not less. This thinking is a reason we invested in Guild, which acts as an education marketplace that helps workers gain skills and improve their careers. Walmart,

The Best Results Come from Leading with Curiosity

Disney, and Chipotle are some of Guild's biggest clients. Guild's software gets inputs about an employee and uses it to understand that person's goals and challenges. Its software absorbs details of the client company's education benefits and cross-references that with a database of schools and courses that the benefits would cover. A Walmart truck driver with a high school education worries that autonomous vehicles will put him out of work; Guild will help him use Walmart's benefits to get a degree that puts him on a more promising career path. And true to our belief in inclusive capitalism, Guild is not just a nice thing to do. It's a good business. Founded in 2015, Guild now has 1,200 employees and a multibillion-dollar valuation.

Leading with generosity is also foundational to our efforts in health assurance. The incumbent healthcare system is anything but equitable. Wealthy people get the best doctors, the best treatments, and the most attention. In part, that's because traditional healthcare is a scarce resource. In that system, typically the only way to get care is to see a medical provider in person, and there aren't enough providers in existence to care for everyone who needs them. Demand far exceeds supply, so the cost goes up and the most sought-after providers can choose to charge a lot, eschew insurance, and only see rich people.

One goal of health assurance is to use technology to create abundance in healthcare, altering the equation of supply and demand. Hippocratic AI can give everyone an AI healthcare agent to talk to. Out of a severe shortage of healthcare professionals, the technology can create abundance. The cost of care comes down and becomes more accessible to more people.

With the same health equity purpose in mind, we funded Homeward to make good healthcare more affordable and

The Transformation Principles

accessible in rural areas. As Homeward CEO Jennifer Schneider says, access to care is a big issue when someone lives far from a clinic or hospital. "When you need to see a doctor, you have to drive multiple hours for a fifteen-minute visit. If you're an hourly wage worker, it's not actually an unreasonable decision to not do it. You're giving up a full day of pay to go for a fifteen-minute visit."[36] So Homeward parks a provider van outside the local post office or sets a temporary office up in the corner of a pharmacy, taking healthcare to the people who need it. Homeward is not a charitable organization—it's potentially a multibillion-dollar business.

Curiosity and generosity have been essential in our acquisition of Summa Health, a community health system that operates in five counties across northeast Ohio. The community was understandably wary. Our goal is to make Summa a proving ground for technology and practices that can make care more abundant, affordable, and equitable. We couldn't go in saying we have all the answers. "We let the community know we are here to listen and understand their challenges and collaborate on a transformational plan," says Marc Harrison, who runs the business unit General Catalyst set up for these health assurance operations. "When you sit with the board you're immediately reminded that this system is the most important player in the community. It's where families have gone for healthcare for over two hundred years. We have to be sensitive to these issues. We have to be maximally impactful but minimally disruptive. Rule number one is: Don't break the place."[37] If Marc and the rest of us lead with curiosity and generosity, we will collaborate with the community to make care better and more accessible for everyone in the region, and that will win us permission to pursue our goals

The Best Results Come from Leading with Curiosity

of showing the world how technology can change the nature of healthcare for the better.

I also founded a non-profit called the Health Assurance Foundation, which is focused on programs that make healthcare more equitable and inclusive across all types of communities. When we found or fund a health assurance company, those companies can choose to donate some equity to the foundation, and most do. As of this writing, the foundation has just over $130 million in assets.

The only way to generate massive change is to create movements, and movements only happen when generous leaders show the way and develop followers. Such leaders adhere to the transformation principles in this book. They begin with a soul devoted to the cause. They see a new future and find a way to take us there through constant ambiguity. They play their own new and exciting game. They collaborate with the stakeholders around them—not try to disrupt and alienate them. They understand the interplay between the context they're in and human nature. They lead with curiosity and generosity. And they believe in making inclusive capitalism a force for good, trusting that positive impact and enduring returns go together.

Making General Catalyst into a new kind of entity that generates and nurtures innovative, enduring, positive-impact companies has been my most important goal. Responsible innovation is at the heart of our mission, our relationships, and our approach to building businesses. We believe that for companies to endure, they must continue to innovate and align with the long-term interests of society. As investors and company builders, we can no longer engineer solely for growth; we must embrace the right constraints, transparency, and framework to engineer for growth and good—for impact plus returns.

EPILOGUE

HOW THE TRANSFORMATION PRINCIPLES APPLY TO AI

I'm writing this book in the middle of an unprecedented time of possibilities and change, which at the same time is giving people around the world both great hope and great anxiety.

Artificial intelligence technology is moving and improving so quickly, it's almost impossible to keep up. In many ways, this is exciting. We human beings are developing a technology that has the power to help us solve many of our hardest problems. It could spin out innovations that reverse climate change, cure cancer, end poverty, and make war less likely. Yet it also could backfire. If AI eliminates vast numbers of jobs, people will be miserable, left without a purpose. AI can create convincing misinformation that manipulates whole populations or maybe dupes us into starting wars.

With the pace of change so great, and with so much at stake, it becomes even more important to base decisions about AI innovations on a set of transformation principles. The principles act as a guide, helping to sort through the confusion and make good choices.

There's nothing more essential right now for General

The Transformation Principles

Catalyst—and for me—than to make good decisions about AI. Such decisions will determine our company's future and perhaps the planet's future. We have an opportunity to reinvent whole industries for the better, and we don't want to screw it up.

So, I thought it would be useful to lay out how the transformation principles in this book help us shape our thinking and actions around AI. We may not get everything right all the time, but we believe our principles help us get decisions more right than wrong.

For the purposes of this book, the transformation principles are presented in order, but in real life things don't work that way. Different situations require applying the principles in a different order, and sometimes some of the principles apply but not all, and sometimes several principles come into play all at once.

In the case of powerful new generations of AI that burst into our lives in 2022, our application of the transformation principles started with serendipity, which our company needed to turn into intentionality.

Serendipity Must Become Intentional

The serendipity that landed on our industry was the unleashing of the awesome power of large language model AIs such as OpenAI's ChatGPT and Mistral's 7B. Artificial intelligence technology had been around for decades, and it was already driving a reimagining of sectors like healthcare and finance. I even wrote about how AI will transform major industries in my book (also with Kevin Maney) *Unscaled*, which came out in 2018. But not a lot of people in our industry expected such a sudden acceleration of the

How the Transformation Principles Apply to AI

technology. In what seemed like a flash, new possibilities for applications and companies opened up. As VCs, we were in a perfect position to fund or start some of these companies.

It could've been tempting to adopt a gold-rush mentality—to get in on building anything we could think of with generative AI. Some in the tech ecosystem have wanted to let AI run wild and see what works and what doesn't—then shut down what doesn't work and build on what does. But we felt that could be dangerous and ultimately slow the progress of AI if and when something were to go wrong. Let's say we try to "move fast and break things" and unleash a medical AI application into the world that hasn't been deeply trained and vetted, and it starts giving bad advice and someone dies. Lawsuits would get filed, and regulators would clamber to shut it down, setting the technology back.

Our intentional approach at General Catalyst has been to take time to understand where AI can have an important positive impact and build companies and responsible technology aimed at those opportunities. Hippocratic AI is an example. We believed that generative AI opened up the possibility of relieving the nursing shortage that has plagued healthcare since the COVID-19 pandemic. But a healthcare AI can't be allowed to make mistakes or draw on bad information. Hippocratic AI must be responsible about what it is building. It's difficult and expensive to train an AI so it becomes thorough and free of mistakes, but Hippocratic AI committed to spending more than a year on training (with data and with the help of doctors and nurses) before even releasing a trial version. Building trust with the clinical workforce to allow the AI workforce to do some of their work was an essential step in bringing Hippocratic AI to the market.

This principle about intentionality guided us to go against

The Transformation Principles

some opinions in the tech sphere and be proponents of collaborating with regulators on thoughtful governance of AI. For some in the VC community, that's been a highly controversial point. They mistake "self-regulation" for slowing progress and inviting regulation, when the true intent is to build trust with regulators to level the playing field for new companies, which is essential for accelerating progress. The idea that society will allow AI innovators to pursue their visions without any input is naive. We're committed to building trust with society at large during this next stage of rapid transformation that stands to unlock so much good in the world.

The Business Must Have a Soul

As we look at AI opportunities, there are really two souls at play: ours at General Catalyst and the souls inside the founders who want to work with us.

As described in many ways in this book, our soul at General Catalyst is rooted in a desire to drive powerful positive change that endures. We have faith that positive impact leads to the best returns. Our soul is committed to the transformation principles in this book. All of that guides our decisions about AI.

First, by following our soul, we knew we had to be major players in building AI-driven companies, because it is obvious that AI has the potential to reinvent industries for the better, which aligns with our mission. Plus, as capitalists, investing in AI-driven reinvention is an enormous opportunity that we can't miss.

Second, our soul guides us to make sure our actions are not just about building AI companies to cash in on this wave but

How the Transformation Principles Apply to AI

instead are aimed at building responsible, impactful AI companies that will solve hard problems and endure for the long run.

Our soul helps us stay committed to our approach, even if others in technology espouse a different path. Our soul gives us the strength to stay the course, believing we will be right in the long run.

Because we are committed to the transformation principles, and one of those principles is that companies must have a soul, ultimately we only want to engage with companies that have a soul rooted in the problem they are addressing.

We have no interest in a founder who wants to build an AI business because AI businesses are hot and a path to making quick money. I learned that lesson when I tried to cash in on the mobile boom with my first company—and failed. We want to work with founders whose souls drive them to fix an important problem any way they can and who see AI as a means to that end. A founder with a soul is building a company because that company will become his or her life's mission.

In other words, amid the frenzy about AI, our principles tell us to stick with founders who build companies with a soul and reject those who don't.

Creating the Future Beats Improving the Past

The arrival of powerful new generations of AI gives our company a chance to play a role in transforming industries for the better. We're not interested in tinkering around the edges. For most of the existence of the digital technology industry, technology typically made what we already did more efficient—faster,

The Transformation Principles

easier, cheaper. Software let accountants add and track numbers much faster, but it didn't change accounting all that much. Online banking let consumers be more efficient—no more need to waste time driving to the bank to deposit a check—and helped banks save money on bank branches and labor, but it didn't fundamentally transform banking.

This AI era is different. We want to get involved with companies that make us think differently about whole industries, about the nature of work and management, or about manufacturing or commerce or health or purpose. More than ever, the filter for founders coming to General Catalyst now is: Blow our minds. That means creating a new future, not making the past more efficient.

Hippocratic AI is, again, a worthy example. For decades, companies have sold software and gadgets that could make nursing more efficient. Medical records got digitized so nurses didn't have to flip through paper files. Software could make scheduling faster than doing it manually. But if Hippocratic AI can put an AI healthcare agent in everyone's pocket, making some of what nurses do abundant, it literally changes how we think about patients getting the care they need. It opens up a new future that we couldn't have seen just a couple of years earlier.

The principle of creating a new future also applies to General Catalyst, not just the companies we found or fund. Our most robust effort has been in the AI-driven transformation of healthcare into health assurance. Most VC firms fund an interesting company here and another one there, but huge and complex sectors like healthcare won't be transformed by any individual company. If we live by a principle of creating a new future, then we must think about how to organize our investments and activities to have a great enough impact to move all of healthcare from an old,

How the Transformation Principles Apply to AI

broken model to a new, transformational model. And that means that we can't just hope that founders with good ideas come to us. If we see a way that technology and AI can move along the transformation of healthcare, and we're not seeing founders propose it, we'll start that company ourselves. That's what we did with Commure, for instance. And then, in 2024, we took the radical step—for a VC firm—of buying a health system so we can prove out new technologies and new ways of thinking about healthcare.

By 2024, we had well over 100 portfolio companies in healthcare, all working on reinventing different parts of the ecosystem. If we want to help the healthcare ecosystem transform into health assurance, it won't happen if we just build a portfolio of a few interesting companies. We have to marshal a small army of companies behind a cohesive strategy.

As our company takes aim at the transformation of other sectors—including energy and finance—we will apply the principle of creating a new future. If we're only improving the past, we shouldn't bother. As a company, we have to be all in on creating a new future in big, complex sectors that badly need transformation for the good of us all. So, like our work on health assurance, we will take a holistic, organized approach to creating and proving out innovations that, when taken together, move a sector from the past to a new future.

Those Who Play Their Own Game Win

In our approach to AI and building a new future, we believe General Catalyst is playing its own game. We're not following the venture capital playbook.

The Transformation Principles

In January 2022, well before the generative AI explosion, I published the book *Intended Consequences* about responsible innovation—especially the responsible development of AI. Around the same time, I helped start Responsible Innovation Labs. It's a nonprofit set up to bring investors, founders, scientists, and policymakers together to rally around responsible AI and share best practices. Dozens of VC firms and companies have signed a set of responsible AI commitments that RI Labs drafted.

Some of the most prominent VC firms in the tech ecosystem didn't share our position and instead advocated for a "let 'er rip" approach to AI. Playing our own game helped General Catalyst make a name for itself as a principled, long-term steward of AI, and that has helped bring us the kind of founders we want to work with.

Another way we have played our own game: Most VC firms only *invest* in companies. General Catalyst is one of the only VCs that also partners with founders to *start* category-defining companies. If we see a company or technology that must exist in the world but doesn't, we'll work with fantastic entrepreneurs to start a company to solve that problem. Long ago, we were involved in starting Kayak in the travel space. Then we helped build Demandware, which Salesforce bought. Once we got on the path of transforming healthcare, we helped start Livongo and then Commure. Now, as we look at what new generations of AI can do, we will partner to start AI companies that we believe are needed to transform a sector. (While this trait is part of us playing our own game as a VC company, we also only work to start companies that play their own game. We will never start a copycat company.)

In the 2020s, General Catalyst has been transforming into a unique kind of enduring innovation-creation company. If we

How the Transformation Principles Apply to AI

want to reinvent healthcare in the United States, or solve climate change, the venture capital model doesn't work because it is relying on 10-year funds to try to solve 30- or 50-year problems. So we've been creating a marriage, as I described earlier, of venture capital that can take risks on new innovations and a longer-horizon part of the company that can operate and invest in companies for enduring returns. As far as I know, no entity like us exists. This is our own game.

As you can imagine, this principle of playing our own game applies to founders who come to us wanting to build AI-driven innovations. We want our minds blown by an AI company with a plan to solve an important problem in an entirely new way—a company that will establish and define a new category. We're less interested in investing in AI companies that follow someone else into a category with the promise of doing that thing a little faster or cheaper or better. Instead, category winners tend to be different, playing a one-of-a-kind game. Those are the companies, like Amazon or Tesla in previous decades, that transform an industry, profoundly transform the way we live and work, and throw off enduring returns.

Navigating Ambiguity Is More Valuable Than Predicting the Future

The future of anything that has to do with AI is utterly unpredictable. All we as a society know is that AI is evolving rapidly, and we expect it to have an enormous impact—possibly a greater impact in a shorter time than any technology ever developed.

When a founder of an AI company pitches us for funding, we

The Transformation Principles

constantly remind ourselves of this unpredictability. Yes, we want to get involved with founders who see a new way to use AI to make a powerful positive impact. We want founders who believe in a better future where AI solves an important problem. But no one can possibly know how to get to that future. We have to believe that the founder's primary goal is to solve the problem—the goal can't be to do it in a specific way with a specific technology. The technology will change too much.

So we have to believe in the goal. Some examples: to put an AI healthcare agent in everyone's pocket (Hippocratic AI); to give every kid an education they love (ClassDojo); to help everyone communicate better (Grammarly); to change the nature of war so it deters war (Anduril). At the same time we have to be convinced that the founders aren't wedded to a particular way to get there. We need to believe that the founders will find a way to their goal despite constant twists and turns in technology and the world around them. Those are the founders we can get behind.

Internally at General Catalyst, we embrace this principle too. We have a goal of transforming the existing, costly, frustrating healthcare system into a system that leverages AI and other technology to keep us as healthy as possible so we require as little medical attention as possible. We call that new version of healthcare "health assurance." We fund companies that we think will help get us there. We're buying a health system to help us test and prove the innovations our companies develop. And we know this is a long journey. We will constantly have to adjust, and some of our assumptions may be wrong.

We don't know what the future will be, but we do know that

How the Transformation Principles Apply to AI

healthcare is a vitally important problem to solve, and we're intent on applying whatever technology comes along to solve it.

For Great Change, Radical Collaboration Beats Disruption

For a lot of people, AI seems threatening. Company leaders wonder how it will change their businesses, or whether it will put them out of business. Workers of all kinds—from lawyers to marketers, artists, store clerks, and truck drivers—worry that AI or AI-driven robots will take their jobs.

Yes, AI brings with it the possibility of massive positive transformation of every business sector. Yet if the tech ecosystem goes into any of these sectors with the old Silicon Valley message of disruption—like, "We're going to make traditional trucking companies obsolete"—we will run headlong into resistance. Imagine hundreds of thousands of truck drivers marching on Washington, demanding the banning of autonomous trucks. Imagine Fortune 500 CEOs organizing industry groups and lobbying efforts to tightly regulate AI; and finding a receptive audience of policymakers who fear seeing whole corporations collapse and their communities devastated.

The tech industry would be better served by collaborating instead of trying to disrupt. And that's never been more true than in this era of AI. Whether it's General Catalyst or an individual AI startup, we have to go to incumbent companies and industries with a message of collaboration and helpfulness: We're going to help you build these technologies and become AI enabled, and

The Transformation Principles

we'll do it in a responsible way because you do have to think about workforce transformation and the impact on your communities.

We need to tell incumbents that they should consider all their stakeholders. If companies embrace AI in service of one stakeholder but ignore the adverse effect on others, those companies will suffer a backlash. We also need to think about AI's impact on more than just shareholders, employees, and customers, but on the broader context in which we all operate. If the AI transformation leads to a chaotic, divided, broken society... well, that won't be good for any kind of business.

All of this factors into our decisions about AI investments and company building. We want to be involved with companies that have a radical collaboration mindset. We want companies that stand ready to work with incumbents and help them adopt AI-driven innovations that can transform an industry for the better. Companies that collaborate stand a better chance of enduring and generating compounding returns. They stand a better chance of helping society transform in a positive way instead of a destructive way.

By thinking expansively about society's well-being, we also see new opportunities for company creation. If one startup develops AI that can power a fully automated driverless trucking industry, that will create new problems that must be solved, such as how to retrain displaced drivers, what to do with masses of outdated nonautomated trucks, or how to refuel autonomous trucks along their routes. New problems become openings for new categories of products and services. At General Catalyst, we think holistically about transformation and want to make sure all the pieces are available to make these transformations positive for society.

How the Transformation Principles Apply to AI

Context Constantly Changes, but Human Nature Stays the Same

Context constantly changes, but rarely has it changed so much so fast. As we chart our course in AI, we want to work with founders who are eager to play a role in the two seismic shifts in context today. One is technological; the other, geopolitical.

AI is a massive context shift. It comes at a time when we're also developing a number of other powerful technologies, including blockchain, genome editing, robotics, and 3D printing. Whatever we think the future is today will likely seem naive a few years out.

Along with that shift is an ongoing reorienting of the geopolitical context. The 2020 pandemic broke supply chains. Growing nationalism and isolationism made nations rethink their reliance on other nations, and many are trying to build up their resilience and ability to self-sustain. That means that the way our portfolio companies scale and become global is radically changing.

We're also watching how these enormous context shifts might shape AI itself. Every major country wants to have its own AI strategy, and they want their cultural nuances to be implemented in how their AI works. China has already approved more than forty AI models that meet the Chinese government's requirement to "uphold the core socialist values." This trend leads to the risk that AI will become siloed, which is the opposite of how the internet got built with one global standard. We're pushing for countries to collaborate to agree on a common set of frameworks, but that may not be how things turn out.

As General Catalyst looks at AI opportunities, we find it

The Transformation Principles

important to understand and monitor the shifts in context. We regularly meet with scientists, academics, policymakers, and global thinkers so we as a company have an understanding of the context shifts and their implications. The better we understand this, the better we can see what kinds of innovations the world needs, and the better we can evaluate the chances of startups that pitch to us.

Anduril is a terrific example of an AI-driven company that understands both the geopolitical and technological context shifts and is aiming for the opportunity those shifts create. Such companies have a better chance at enduring success than startups that fail to take context shifts into account.

As described earlier in this book, Anduril is also realistic about human nature, which doesn't change. Conflict, jealousy, envy, desire—these aspects of human nature will endure. We can all hope war will become obsolete, but it won't. Instead, Anduril and companies like it are working to make war so unlikely to succeed that it's not worth it. Or if wars are destined to occur, then the goal is to put machines in danger instead of humans.

The concept that human nature doesn't change is a filter we apply to startups that come our way. We want to know that founders have thought through what humans, being humans, will do with their innovations. We often tell AI startups: Now that you've told us what could go right, tell us what could go wrong. How will you keep the worst of human nature from using what you've built to harm society? And how do we make sure we have a governance model that prevents as much of that as possible? In this era of such powerful AI, there's probably no more important question to explore.

We're also aware that it's human nature to want to move fast, grab onto opportunities, and worry about the consequences for later. So we've been telling founders—and ourselves—to stop and think and let's build AI products and services very intentionally.

The Choice Between Positive Impact and Returns Is False

When we're evaluating an AI opportunity, we toggle through all the previous principles, but then we get to the one most profound question:

Will this company have a powerful positive impact?

We have to believe it will. We aren't right every time. But that's a reason we've married the venture capital model (a system of taking risks on innovations) with a long-term investment and operating model (a system of transformation). The VC model is set up for taking chances on promising startups, with the expectation that some will fall short and a few will become multibillion-dollar enduring successes. The successes will enter our system of transformation and become part of a portfolio of companies that help create a new future for an industry such as healthcare, defense, or finance.

Ultimately, our core belief as a company is that companies that set out to drive powerful positive change have the best chance of generating the best long-term returns. Positive impact leads to great returns, and recurring great returns give the company the capital to continue its positive impact, keeping the flywheel going.

This principle also circles back to the spirituality, rooted in my Hindu upbringing, that I apply to my business process. As you know by now, I believe this life is one part of a long journey that

The Transformation Principles

stretches out before and after. It's important to me to build companies that are on a similarly long journey—companies that will last for generations and continue to have a positive impact long after I've left the scene. The rewards that come from following this principle are both financial and spiritual.

The Best Results Come from Leading with Curiosity and Generosity

As AI barrels into society, I'm more aware than ever that the venture capital business needs to change if we want permission from society to be stewards of this powerful technology. While our potential to transform society with innovation is at an all-time high, society's trust in us to do that responsibly is at an all-time low. The public too often sees VCs as a bunch of "tech bros" who get rich by funding companies that either exploit the working class or automate middle-class jobs away with AI. If we're going to change that perception, we need to lead with curiosity and generosity.

Curiosity means having a beginner's mind and an open mind. I try to go into every meeting with an AI startup with the humility to say that I don't know how this innovation will impact the market and society. VCs are, essentially, selling money, and the power of that can make someone in this business believe their own point of view about how the technology is going to work or what impact it will have. But AI is changing so fast, and creating so many potential opportunities, that no one could possibly have all the answers. To be effective and be a good steward of AI, we VCs have to disengage from our "knowledge" and instead evaluate companies through sound principles. As long as those

How the Transformation Principles Apply to AI

principles include some of the ones in this book—have a soul; create a new future; understand context and human nature; build for impact plus returns—we'll make better decisions for society and for future generations.

As for generosity, venture capital has created astounding wealth over the past 50 years. But it has not shown as much interest in creating an equitable or healthy society. VCs have long operated on 10-year cycles—our charters call for us to invest, build, and exit within a decade. Exiting and making money for limited partners has long been the VC endgame. In most cases, a company's VC investors wash their hands of a company after the exit. If a company does as much harm as good, well, sorry, but at least early investors had a good exit.

That has to change in the AI era. The technologies are too powerful. The potential for harm or unintended consequences is far too great. And if AI is going to truly transform whole industries, it will take longer than a 10-year VC cycle. We have to play the long game now and do it with society's well-being in mind.

Venture capital has to move from a goal of exit to a goal of endure—a future where inclusive capitalism prioritizes impact plus returns and is a mechanism for enduring positive outcomes. That twist in outlook will help turn our focus to funding positive change, which will in turn help win the public's trust. At GC, the same LPs who greatly benefited from our past returns are asking to play a role in building companies in a more inclusive way. In the last wave of productivity, most of the value was captured by a handful of tech companies like Microsoft and Alphabet. In this AI wave, we and our partners want to be intentional about how productivity gains accrue to everyone.

Generosity means actively working to build a more equitable

world. The wealth the tech ecosystem generates tends to go to an elite layer of society. Now our industry is building AI that will automate jobs away. If we don't manage this transition with generosity and make sure people have meaningful work and meaningful wealth, we'll exacerbate already-dangerous societal divides. The gap between the 1% and the rest of the population will widen into a canyon. That would be destabilizing.

As I write this, capitalism and democratic societies are under threat all over the globe, including in the United States. If the stewards of AI act with generosity now, we stand a chance of continuing to have society's permission to do business and create innovations in the coming decades.

Acknowledgments

I want to start by thanking my family—my wife, Jessica, and our three wonderful children, Ajay, Arya, and Isabella, for allowing me to dedicate so much of my energy toward my mission at General Catalyst.

Next, I want to thank my mother, Santosh, whose own quest for spirituality in life has been foundational to making it mine in business.

I am grateful for my now decade-long partnership with Kevin Maney, as this is our fourth book together, and one that required a lot of patience from him as I went down my own self-discovery path to be able to write it.

I also want to thank my colleague Drake Pooley, whose doggedness in helping me focus, reflect, and refine the core points was essential to getting this manuscript finished.

Lastly, I want to thank everyone who shared stories about their work, including my General Catalyst partners Jeannette zu Fürstenberg and Pranav Singhvi, and founders who are part of the General Catalyst portfolio.

Notes

1. "The Richest American Men Live 15 Years Longer Than the Poorest Men, While the Richest American Women Live 10 years Longer Than the Poorest Women." See The Equality of Opportunity Project, accessed March 27, 2025, http://www.equality-of-opportunity.org/health/.
2. Nick Romeo, "Debating Economic Inequality, with Help from Jesus, Plato and Rousseau," *The Washington Post*, September 22, 2024, https://www.washingtonpost.com/books/2024/09/22/greatest-all-plagues-income-inequality-jesus-plato-david-lay-williams-review/.
3. More about this in the *Harvard Business Review* article "Geopolitics Are Changing. Venture Capital Must, Too," by Hemant Taneja and Fareed Zakaria, published on February 10, 2023.
4. Thomas J. Watson Jr., *A Business and Its Beliefs: The Ideas That Helped Build IBM* (McGraw-Hill, 1963), 5.
5. Interview with Mukesh Chatter for this section by the authors, 2024.
6. Interview with Qasar Younis by the authors, 2023.
7. Interview with Toyin Ajayi by the authors, 2023.
8. Centers for Medicare & Medicaid Services, "NHE Fact Sheet," accessed March 21, 2025, https://www.cms.gov/data-research/statistics-trends-and-reports/national-health-expenditure-data/nhe-fact-sheet.
9. Interview with Zach Reitano for this section by the authors, 2023.
10. Kevin Maney, "The King of Alter Egos Is Surprisingly Humble Guy," *USA Today*, February 5, 2007, accessed January 20, 2025, https://

Notes

usatoday30.usatoday.com/printedition/money/20070205/secondlife_cover.art.htm.

11. Todd Spangler, "Netflix Wins Six Oscars, Including for 'All Quiet on the Western Front,' Guillermo del Toro's 'Pinocchio,'" *Variety*, March 12, 2023, https://variety.com/2023/awards/news/netflix-2023-oscars-wins-all-quiet-on-the-western-front-pinocchio-1235544587/.
12. Interview with Zach Reitano by the authors, 2023.
13. Interview with Sanit Biswas for this section by the authors, 2023.
14. Jerome Roos, "We Don't Know What Will Happen Next," *The New York Times*, April 28, 2023, https://www.nytimes.com/2023/04/18/opinion/global-crisis-future.html.
15. Interview with Brian Schimpf for this section by the authors, 2023.
16. Interview with Sam Chaudhary for this section by the authors, 2024.
17. Interview with Brad Hoover for this section by the authors, 2022.
18. Interviews with Munjal Shah for this section by the authors, 2023 and 2024.
19. Jeff St. John, "Gridco Shuts Down Its Digital Grid Controls Business," *Greentech Media*, January 18, 2018, https://www.greentechmedia.com/articles/read/gridco-shuts-down-its-digital-grid-controls-business.
20. Interview with Jennifer Schneider for this section by the authors, 2023.
21. Interview with Qasar Younis by the authors, 2023.
22. Interview with Torsten Reil for this section by the authors, 2024.
23. Interview with Jeff Wilke for this section by Kevin Maney, 2024.
24. Robert Waldinger and Marc Shulz, *The Good Life: Lessons from the World's Longest Scientific Study of Happiness* (Simon & Schuster, 2023), 24.
25. Interview with Torsten Reil by the authors, 2024.
26. Interview with Brian Schimpf by the authors, 2023.
27. Interview with Andy Lee for this section by the authors, 2024.
28. Interviews with Priyanka Agarwal by the authors, 2023 and 2024.
29. Interview with Siva Yellamraju for this section by the authors, 2024.
30. Interviews with Peter Reinhardt by the authors, 2021 and 2024.
31. Peter Reinhardt, "Charm Industrial Could Add Up to 200,000 Jobs to US Economy by 2040," *Charm Industrial* (blog), September 7, 2023, https://charmindustrial.com/blog/charm-industrial-could-add-up-to-200-000-jobs-to-us-economy-by-2040.
32. "Servant Leadership Theory," post on Harvard Law School

Notes

Program on Negotiation site: https://www.pon.harvard.edu/daily/leadership-skills-daily/servant-leadership-theory/.
33. Glenn Rifkin, "Herb Kelleher, Whose Southwest Airlines Reshaped the Industry, Dies at 87," *The New York Times*, January 3, 2019, https://www.nytimes.com/2019/01/03/obituaries/herb-kelleher-whose-southwest-airlines-reshaped-the-industry-dies-at-87.html.
34. Jacqueline Molik Ghosen, "Servant Leaders Are Better for the Bottom Line," UBNow, July 25, 2023, https://www.buffalo.edu/ubnow/stories/2023/07/lemoine-servant-leaders.html.
35. Interview with Pranav Singhvi by the authors, 2024.
36. Interview with Jennifer Schneider by the authors, 2023.
37. Interview with Marc Harrison by the authors, 2024.

About the Authors

Hemant Taneja is the CEO and managing director at General Catalyst, the world's foremost investment and transformation company, supporting global resilience through applied AI. He laid out his applied AI thesis in his 2018 book *Unscaled* (with Kevin Maney), which explored how the economy will be shaped by entrepreneurs who use applied AI to drive mass personalization.

Hemant invested early in market leaders such as Stripe, Samsara, Snap, Gitlab, Grammarly, Gusto, Applied Intuition, Anduril, Ro, and Canva.

He's now working to transform healthcare. His 2020 book, *UnHealthcare* (with Stephen Klasko and Kevin Maney), outlined General Catalyst's thesis for how healthcare needs to transform from a "sick care" system into a health assurance system that is proactive, accessible, and affordable. Hemant serves as the founder and chairman of the Health Assurance Transformation Company and helped found health assurance companies Commure, Transcarent, Hippocratic AI, and Livongo.

Hemant has focused his philanthropic time on programs and policies that accelerate transformation of industries where he is actively investing. He helped cofound Responsible Innovation Labs, Advanced Energy United, and Health Assurance Foundation. He helped build Khan Lab School, an innovative K–12 school that his three children attended, and serves as a trustee of Northeastern University and on the Stanford School of Medicine Board of Fellows. Hemant and his wife signed the Giving Pledge in 2024.

Hemant is a graduate of the Massachusetts Institute of Technology, where he earned five degrees.

Kevin Maney is a bestselling author, award-winning columnist, and founding partner at Category Design Advisors (CDA). This is his fourth book in collaboration with Hemant Taneja.

His critically acclaimed book, *Play Bigger: How Pirates, Dreamers and Innovators Create and Dominate Markets*, introduced business to the methodology called "category design." As a founding partner of CDA, Maney has helped leadership teams at hundreds of companies all over the world focus their strategic thinking through category design.

In 2024, Maney published his first novel, *Red Bottom Line*. Set in Moscow in 1991, it's based on his reporting as a journalist covering the breakup of the Soviet Union. His biography, *The*

Maverick and His Machine: Thomas Watson Sr., became the de facto history of IBM.

Maney has been a contributor to *Newsweek*, *Fortune*, *The Atlantic*, *Fast Company*, CNN, and ABC News, among other media outlets. He was a contributing editor at *Conde Nast Portfolio* from 2007 to 2009. For 22 years, he was a columnist, editor, and reporter at *USA Today*.

He's appeared on television and radio, including *CBS Sunday Morning* and NPR, and lectured at conferences and universities, including New York University, the University of North Carolina Chapel Hill, and his alma mater, Rutgers.